Deacon Relationships

Through

The Body of Christ

By

Dr. Donald E. Ledbetter

PRESS

Deacon Relationships Through The Body of Christ
by Dr. Donald E. Ledbetter

Printed in the United States of America

ISBN 978-1-60791-710-6

www.xulonpress.com

Who Is Don Ledbetter?

D r. Don Ledbetter was born in Anniston, Alabama. He and his wife Linda have two sons, Steve and Stan; two precious daughter-in-laws, Cheryl and Angela; and three grandchildren, Alysha, Zachary, and Hannah.

Don has served churches in Alabama and Georgia, most recently Liberty Baptist, now located in Riverdale, Georgia. After a seventeen-year pastoral ministry, Don entered vocational evangelism in January 1984. Since entering evangelism, he has conducted over five hundred revivals and crusades across America. He has preached for the Georgia, Florida, and Tennessee Baptist State Conventions and for numerous associational and area-wide evangelism conferences across the southeast. Don has served two terms as president for the Georgia Baptist Evangelists.

He graduated from Florida Baptist College and Luther Rice University. He earned his doctorate from Luther Rice in 1981.

Don also is an excellent teacher. He has conducted several hundred Harvest Sundays, marriage retreats, deacons' retreats, and Sunday school seminars across America. For four consecutive years, he shared with the students at the New Orleans Theological Seminary campus in Atlanta, Georgia, on the subject, "What an Evangelist Wished Every Pastor Knew About Revival."

Dedication

Without doubt, the ministry of the deacon is one of God's greatest gifts to the church. It has been my joy to serve with some of God's choice deacons over the years. In each of the four churches that I served as pastor, the overwhelming majority of deacons were men of great faith. They served the Lord with valor. It was my joy to know them and serve with them.

This book is dedicated in honor of the deacons who serve on my Evangelistic Board:

- Mr. Alvin Stephenson—Jacksonville, Alabama
- Mr. Leroy Reagin—Brunswick, Georgia
- Mr. Joe Friend—Caldwell, Georgia
- Mr. Jack McCorkle—Dearing, Georgia
- Mr. Barry Davis—Tyrone, Georgia
- Mr. Ozal Evans—Sylvania, Georgia

Forward

From a Pastor:

    Deacon Relationships Through the Body of Christ is a practical and complete guide on the office and work of a deacon. This straightforward and Bible-based book will help any deacon to understand his role and position within the church. Dr. Ledbetter has grounded each of the deacon's relationships scripturally. He will challenge every deacon to his highest potential for the work of the church and the glory of God. *Deacon Relationships* is a <u>must</u>-read book for every deacon.

Jerry Starling, Pastor
Lakeview Baptist Church
Oxford, Alabama

From a Deacon:

This book belongs in the library of every church, pastor, and deacon. *Deacon Relationships Through the Body of Christ* clarifies the role of the deacon in the five basic relationships of the deacon's ministry.

The deacon in relation to Christ
The deacon in relation to his family
The deacon in relation to his church
The deacon in relation to his pastor
The deacon in relation to himself

As Dr. Ledbetter addresses each of these entities, you also will discover spiritual insights that will help you become a better husband, father, friend, and neighbor. If you will implement what this book reveals, you, your family, and your church will be blessed.
You will want to share this book with your friends! I highly recommend it!

Barry Davis
Owner: Cornerstone Financial Services
Tyrone, Georgia

From a Director of Missions:

I have known Brother Don Ledbetter for more than twenty years. He always has been a communicator of high integrity and spiritual depth. His training seminars are of superb quality. Not only gifted as an evangelist, he is able to train leaders and encourage couples as an engaging conference leader. His deacon training is scripturally based, easy to understand, and relevant to this day we live in. I have every confidence that those who read this book will find it challenging and very beneficial.

Rev. Ronald Wildes,
Associational Missionary
Fairburn Baptist Association
Fairburn, Georgia

From a Layman:

Deacon Relationships Through the Body of Christ, is very enlightening for both the deacon and the layman in today's trying times. It addresses the basic relationships of every Christian's life.
1. One's relation to Christ
2. One's relation to his family
3. One's relation to his church
4. One's relation to his pastor
5. One's relation to himself.

In a highly uplifting manner, these principles will be rewarding to everyone that applies them to their life's work. I strongly encourage every church member to study its relevance today.

Gene Evans
Owner: Great South Harley-Davidson
Newnan, Georgia

Table of Contents

Chapter 1

The Deacon in Relation to Christ

As you begin this book, permit me to ask you about your relationship with Christ. Are you a Christian? Does the Holy Spirit control you? To be an effective deacon, you must have a personal relationship with Christ and be controlled by His Spirit. If you are not "right" with Christ, you will not be an effective deacon. Being a Christian involves more than saying, "I believe in Christ," or joining a church and being baptized. True conversion involves a genuine change—a change of heart, a change of mind, and a change of direction. When one is truly saved, his life will show evidence of becoming Christlike. The sad truth is "Christlikeness" is not demonstrated by many in the church today.

Without doubt, the church today is in serious spiritual trouble. I believe the seven churches of Revelation 2 and 3 represent successive periods of time in church history. The Laodicean church (Rev. 3:14-22) represents the church of the last days. Listen to the description of this last day church.

> I know thy works, that thou art neither cold nor hot: I would thou wert cold or hot. So then because thou art lukewarm, and neither cold nor hot, I will spue thee out of my mouth. Because thou sayest, I am rich, and increased with goods, and have need of nothing; and knowest not that thou art wretched, and miserable, and poor, and blind, and naked: I counsel thee to buy of me gold tried in the fire, that thou mayest be rich; and white raiment, that thou mayest be clothed, and that the shame of thy nakedness do not appear; and anoint thine eyes with eyesalve, that thou mayest see. As many as I love, I rebuke and chasten: be zealous therefore, and repent. Behold, I stand at the door, and knock: if any man hear my voice, and open the door, I will come in to him, and will sup with him, and he with me.
>
> —Revelation 3:15-20

What do these verses tell us about the spiritual condition of the church just prior to the coming of Christ? John tells us the church will be in a spiritual state of depravity, lukewarm and indifferent. The majority of the members of this church will view themselves as spiritually sound, lacking nothing. However, this is not the way Christ will see the last-days church. John says Christ will see this church as wretched, laboring but to no avail, void of joy even to the point of being miserable. This church will be poor in spiritual understanding and poor in God's blessings. It will be blind to God's will, unable to see a lost world in need of Christ, and unable to see God's ability to use them to win the lost to Christ. It will see itself, not as it is, but how its members would like for it to be, all the while being spiritually unrobed, without God's holiness and righteousness.

Ask any preacher, "What would you like to have more of in your church?" and he will tell you, "Committed people." Are you as committed to Christ as you should be? If you are looking for an example of a committed man, consider Paul. We see his commitment to Christ in 2 Corinthians 11:24-31:

> Of the Jews five times received I forty stripes save one. Thrice was I beaten with rods, once was I stoned, thrice I suffered shipwreck, a night and a day I have been in the deep; in journeyings often, in perils of waters, in perils of robbers, in perils by mine own countrymen, in perils by the heathen, in perils in the city, in perils in the wilderness, in perils in the sea, in perils among false brethren; in weariness and painfulness, in watchings often, in hunger and thirst, in fastings often, in cold and nakedness. Beside those things that are without, that which cometh upon me daily, the care of all the churches. Who is weak, and I am not weak? who is offended, and I

burn not? If I must needs glory, I will glory of the things which concern mine infirmities. The God and Father of our Lord Jesus Christ, which is blessed for evermore, knoweth that I lie not.

How many Christians do you know that would endure these hardships and remain faithful in their service to Christ? Why was Paul so committed to Christ? It was not because he was brought up in a Christian home. Neither was he committed to Christ because it was the popular thing to do. Paul tells us there were two primary reasons that caused him to commit himself to Christ. The first reason is noted in 2 Corinthians 5:11: "Knowing therefore the terror of the Lord, we persuade men; but we are made manifest unto God; and I trust also are made manifest in your consciences." Paul said he was committed to Christ because he believed in God's *judgment* — *"Knowing therefore the terror of the Lord . . ."*

In 2 Corinthians 5:10, Paul says, "For we must all appear before the judgment seat of Christ; that every one may receive the things done in his body, according to that he hath done, whether it be good or bad." The fact that fear of God's judgment doesn't affect many today is evidenced by the way many are living. Yet, each one of us will one day stand before God and give an account of our life. We will be judged for what we have done with Jesus, what we have allowed Jesus to do though us, for those things we should have done but did not do, every idle word, and those secret things in our lives we hoped no one would ever know about.

Peter also tells us that in the last days many will deny Christ's second coming and God's judgment.

> Knowing this first, that there shall come in the last days scoffers, walking after their own lusts, and saying, Where is the promise of his coming? for since the fathers fell asleep, all things continue as they were from the beginning of the creation. For this they willingly are ignorant of, that by the word of God the heavens were of old, and the earth standing out of the water and in the water: Whereby the world that then was, being overflowed with water, perished: But the heavens and the earth, which are now, by the same word are kept in store, reserved unto fire against the day of judgment and perdition of ungodly men.
>
> —2 Peter 3:3-7

Peter tells us that there will be those in the last days who will turn religion into ridicule, who will make light of God's truth and do all they can to water down and distort God's Word, in order to appease the masses. These scoffers will deny God's promises, seek to dismiss God's power, and will try to defile God's petitions. The consequences of the lifestyle of these individuals will do great harm to the cause of Christ. They will be able to convince many that salvation is obtained by doing good deeds, by being good, and by assuming they are good. It is because of the danger that these scoffers poise that Peter asks the question in 2 Peter 3:11: "Seeing then that all these things shall be dissolved, what manner of persons ought ye to be in all holy conversation and godliness."

The second reason Paul was committed to Christ was *love*. In 2 Corinthians 5:14-15, Paul says, "For the love of Christ constraineth us; because we thus judge, that if one died for all, then were all dead: And that he died for all, that they which live should not henceforth live unto themselves, but unto him which died for them, and rose again." The simple reason Paul loved Christ so much was because he met Christ and came to understand personally just how much God loved him. We read of Paul's conversion in Acts 9:3-6.

> And as he journeyed, he came near Damascus: and suddenly there shined round about him a light from heaven: And he fell to the earth, and heard a voice saying unto him, Saul, Saul, why persecutest thou me? And he said, Who art thou, Lord? And the Lord said, I am Jesus whom thou persecutest: it is hard for thee to kick against the pricks. And he trembling and astonished said, Lord, what wilt thou have me to do? And the Lord said unto him, Arise, and go into the city, and it shall be told thee what thou must do.

From this moment on, Paul's life was forever changed. His love and commitment for Christ only grew stronger as the years passed. Listen to what Paul said as he wrote to encourage the church at Philippi.

> . . . I count all things but loss for the excellency of the knowledge of Christ Jesus my Lord: for whom I have suffered the loss of all things, and do count them but dung, that I may win Christ, and be found in him, not having mine own righteousness, which is of the law, but that which is through the faith of Christ, the righteousness which is of God by faith: That I may know him, and the power of his resurrection, and the fellowship of his sufferings, being made conformable unto his death.
>
> —Philippians 3:8-10

Paul also loved Christ because Christ had changed him. I often make the statement in revival services, "If you have ever been saved, you have been changed!" Paul was on his way to Damascus to persecute Christians when he met Christ. A few days later, he was preaching the love of Christ (Acts 9:20). The change that took place in Paul is also noted in Romans 9:1-3.

> I say the truth in Christ, I lie not, my conscience also bearing me witness in the Holy Ghost, that I have great heaviness and continual sorrow in my heart. For I could wish that myself were accursed from Christ

for my brethren, my kinsmen according to
the flesh.

In these verses, Paul evidences the fact that when
Christ comes into your heart, the love of Christ will
be revealed to others through your life. Christ will
change you, causing you to love what you once hated.
No wonder Paul said, "Examine yourselves, whether
ye be in the faith; prove your own selves. Know ye
not your own selves, how that Jesus Christ is in you,
except ye be reprobates?" (2 Cor. 13:5).

Paul loved the Lord because the Lord had given
his life purpose. In Acts 9:15, at Paul's conversion,
God sent Ananias to tell Paul, ". . . he is a chosen
vessel unto me, to bear my name before the Gentiles,
and kings, and the children of Israel." God did not
promise Paul his service for Him would be easy. To
the contrary, God said, "For I will shew him how
great things he must suffer for my name's sake" (Acts
9:16). Paul remained faithful to Christ despite all the
hardships he endured and was able to say, ". . . for I
have learned, in whatsoever state I am, therewith to
be content" (Phil. 4:11).

What most profess to believe

Considering the spiritual condition of America
today, you must conclude that there are many
Christians who are not as committed as they should
be. I have learned, over the years, that what most
people profess to believe makes little or no difference in the way they live. The spiritual condition of
America today is akin to the spiritual condition of

Israel in the day of Ezekiel. In Ezekiel chapter 22, Ezekiel says the spiritual condition of Israel in his day was sinfully filthy and spiritually dry. Many of Israel's preachers were more interested in self-gratification and material gain than they were in God's will or lost souls. They saw no spiritual needs. They received no spiritual revelations from God. Their ministry was one of the flesh, offering only untempered mortar for the support of men's lives. Their oratorical ministry was an expression of intellectualism, established upon lies. Their motivation was materialism and popularity.

The majority of the laity in Ezekiel's day also failed to meet God's standards. They committed appalling acts toward those whom God loved. Their two distinguishing characteristics were oppression and robbery (Ezek. 22:29). The wealthy oppressed the poor, stealing from the helpless. By their actions toward those in need, they demonstrated that they had long forgotten God's grace for supplying their own needs. The moral fiber of the people had reached rock bottom. Rather than executing justice, the political leaders sought financial wealth and political gain. They accepted bribes and lashed out at those who challenged their authority. This sounds like most politicians of today!

God used Ezekiel to challenge his people. Ezekiel says, "And I sought for a man among them, that should make up the hedge, and stand in the gap before me for the land, that I should not destroy it: but I found none" (Ezek. 22:30). God is looking for men and women today who will measure up to that same challenge.

As a deacon, you are to "stand in the gap and make up the hedge." I have met many godly deacons who serve the Lord faithfully. I also have met a few deacons who shared with me that they were lost and others who lived as though they were lost. One night, a deacon slipped into church late. His behavior was strange. His clothes were dirty. He did not sit where he normally sat. His wife and children were not with him. I noticed those around him giving one another strange looks as he sat down. After the service was over, several who sat near this deacon came and shared with me that he smelled like a brewery.

The next day when I went by his home; his wife met me at the door with a bruise on her face. She said, "Brother Don, I am glad you came today. I am sure you know my husband was drunk at church last night. He has changed over the past few weeks. He spent yesterday drinking. Last night before he went to church he became belligerent and physically abusive. That is how I got this bruise on my face. I don't know what has got into him." I found out later he was having trouble on his job and was fearful of losing everything. Despite the circumstances of life, there is no excuse for any Christian to revert to his old ways.

As an evangelist, I have preached in over eight hundred churches across America. One night, after I preached a revival service, a man approached me and said, "Can I ask you a question?" "Sure," I said. "How can I help you?" He said, "Is it possible that one can know for sure they are saved?" "Before I answer your question," I said, "let me ask you a question. Are you asking about yourself, or are you asking to obtain information to help someone else?" He said, "I am asking about myself. Though I have been a member and a deacon in this church for a number of years, I told this church that I was not a Christian when they ordained me. The fact that I am not saved has been discussed in several deacons' meetings over the years." To be sure I heard him correctly, I asked, "Did you say you were a member of this church and a deacon, and you are not a Christian?" "That's right!" he answered.

When the man told me he was serving as a deacon and was not a Christian, I said, "Sir, this church has done you and the cause of Christ a grave injustice by ordaining you as a deacon. In addition, you have done this church and the cause of Christ a grave injustice by allowing them to ordain you as a deacon. No one can serve Christ as they should, in any capacity, without knowing Him as their Savior and Lord." I used my Bible to share with him how he could become a Christian and have the assurance of salvation. He thanked me, arose, and walked away without making a decision for Christ.

There was a time in my life when I would have had a hard time believing a church could do such a foolish thing as to ordain an unsaved man as a deacon. However, today such foolishness has become a common practice in churches. A pastor shared with me recently that when his church was choosing new deacons, several members submitted names of men who had not been to church in more than five years. When one of the members was questioned regarding why she submitted the name of one of those men, she replied, "I thought if he was elected a deacon, he would start back to church and get his life right with the Lord." How foolish!

In the first deacons' meeting in a church I served as pastor, I asked, "Are all the deacons of the church present in our meeting today?" 'Two are missing," was the reply. "Who are the two men missing, and do you know why they are not present?" I asked. Another deacon responded, "One is not here because he is angry at the former pastor. The other deacon has never been faithful. I can't remember the last time he was at church for a worship service or at a deacons' meeting." When I asked what they were doing to help these men understand their responsibilities as a deacon, the chairman of deacons said, "What do you recommend we do?" I said, "I believe it is the responsibility of every organization and committee within the church to discipline themselves. When a member of an organization or committee cannot or will not serve as required, the chairman and co-chairman should visit that person and help them understand their position is not an honorary title but an awesome responsibility."

The chairman and co-chairman of deacons visited these two men, and before our next deacons' meeting, both men resigned. The angry deacon was unwilling to deal with his anger. The slothful deacon sent the deacons a message, stating, "No one has the right to tell me how I should live."

I have had the great joy and privilege of serving with many deacons who have loved the Lord and served Him in ways that brought honor to His name. They encouraged their pastor, enriched their church, enlightened the spiritual life of their family, and through their witness, invited their community to know Christ as their Savior. God, in His wisdom, did a great day's work when He gave the office of the deacon to the church. Truly blessed is the church to have men serve as deacons who do not see themselves as a "Board of Deacons," but as servants of Christ and His church. A church is blessed to have deacons who view their pastor as God's under-shepherd to the church and view their ministry as helping the pastor move the church from where it is spiritually to where Christ would have it be.

What is the role of the deacon's wife?

There were no spiritual rights or privileges afforded the deacon's wife when her husband was ordained a deacon. However, she has every right to believe that when the church selected and elected her husband to be a deacon, her Christianity and character came under scrutiny along with her husband. Thus, she can logically assume that the church saw in her the potential of a godly woman who would be an asset to her husband and his ministry. The role of the deacon's wife is of vital importance to the church. Her primary responsibility is to assist her husband as he performs his responsibilities.

I have heard the statement made, "What is shared in the deacons' meetings is not to be shared with the deacon's wife." I disagree! She is a vital part of her husband's ministry. If her husband informs her of what is shared in the deacons' meetings, she is better able to pray with him about these issues. However, the information her husband shares with her should be received and handled with discretion. She is not to gossip or use the information she receives from her husband in a way that would be harmful to individuals or the church as a whole. If she is living for Christ as she should, she can be of great value to both her husband and the church.

It is as important for the deacon's wife to be saved and Spirit-filled as it is for the deacon, although I am aware that this is not always the case. Being unfaithful to church services, dressing inappropriately, being unfriendly, gossiping, and being publicly negative about her church and pastor cause harm to her husband, her church, and the cause of Christ. In this case, she must be made aware of the destructive effects of her actions, and a visit from other deacons' wives to help her better understand her role would be appropriate.

One Sunday morning, God blessed the invitation in a special way. Among other decisions made that morning, thirty-two made professions of faith. Two of those who accepted Christ as their Savior were deacons' wives. The first woman said, "Brother Don, I am the W.M.U. director in our church, the teacher of a women's Sunday school class, and the wife of a deacon. I am coming this morning to share with you that I am lost. For as long as I can remember, I have wanted to acknowledge my spiritual condition. I have been ashamed to tell others I am not a Christian. I have not come forward before, because I have been afraid of embarrassing my husband. I thought I could find peace by working in the church, but that has not worked. I am sorry for living a lie. This morning I am coming to ask Christ, you, and the church to forgive me. I want to be saved." She was saved that morning, and her life demonstrated a new love for Christ.

When the first lady turned to walk away, another deacon's wife stepped forward. As she took my hand, she said, "Brother Don, when my husband was ordained twenty-five years ago, I was asked if I was a Christian. I said I was, but I was not. I told a story. I have been reluctant to come forward over the years because of my foolish pride. I also have been fearful of embarrassing my husband and family. This morning, I have concluded that I am not going to hell because of what others might think about me. If I embarrass my husband or children, they will get over it. I want to be saved." She too accepted Christ that morning.

Examine your life

I have shared with you about some lost and carnal deacons and deacons' wives in order to challenge you to examine your own life. Are you saved and Spirit-filled? Let me remind you again of what Paul says in 2 Corinthians 13:5, "Examine yourselves, whether ye be in the faith; prove your own selves. Know ye not your own selves, how that Jesus Christ is in you, except ye be reprobates?"

In 1 Corinthians 2:14 through 3:6, Paul indentifies three types of people. First, he identifies the *lost person.* He says of the lost person, "But the natural man receiveth not the things of the Spirit of God: for they are foolishness unto him: neither can he know them, because they are spiritually discerned" (1 Cor. 2:14). This verse teaches that a lost person has not acknowledged their sinful condition and invited Christ to forgive them of their sin and live within their heart. The lost person believes they have the right to choose their own path, for the things of God are foolish to them. Paul reminds us that the reason the lost person does not know and cannot know the things of God is ". . . because the things of God are spiritually discerned" (1 Cor. 2:14). God has tried to share His truths with the lost, but they have refused to hear and accept His truths.

The second type of person Paul identifies is the *spiritual person.* Paul says of the spiritual person, "But he that is spiritual judgeth all things, yet he himself is judged of no man. For who hath known the mind of the Lord, that he may instruct him? but we have the mind of Christ" (1 Cor. 2:15, 16). This verse shares that the saved person has judged his life from Christ's point of view. He has acknowledged his guilt of sin and has asked Christ to forgive him. Paul reminds us in Romans 8:1, "There is therefore now no condemnation [no more judgment] to them which are in Christ Jesus, who walk not after the flesh, but after the Spirit."

The third type of person Paul speaks about is the *carnal person.* The word *carnal* is translated from the Greek word *sarkikos,* which means "fleshly." In this context, Paul says more about the carnal person than the lost and spiritual person combined. We also note that Paul addresses the carnal person as "brethren"—a term he uses almost exclusively to refer to Christians. Without examining all that Paul says of the carnal person in chapter three, I want to draw your attention to 1 Corinthians 3:1-3.

> And I, brethren, could not speak unto you as unto spiritual, but as unto carnal, even as unto babes in Christ. I have fed you with milk, and not with meat: for hitherto ye were not able to bear it, neither yet now are ye able. For ye are yet carnal: for whereas there is among you envying, and strife, and divisions, are ye not carnal, and walk as men?

Although a Christian can be, for a time, carnal, a true Christian will not remain carnal for a lifetime. Such a concept is unbiblical. James 2 makes it clear that genuine faith always results in works. Ephesians 2:8-10 declares that we are saved by grace through faith, not by works. However, our salvation will produce works. These verses describe the carnal person as one saved, but one who no longer allows the Lord to control their life. The actions of the carnal Christian are often childish. The desire of the flesh controls the carnal person, who is filled with pride, easily angered, and quick to be offended or to offend. The carnal person is uncommitted and unconcerned about spiritual matters. Though they may appear happy, a carnal person is devoid of joy,

33

for Christian joy comes from serving Christ. Jesus says in John 15:10-11:

> If ye keep my commandments, ye shall abide in my love; even as I have kept my Father's commandments, and abide in his love. These things have I spoken unto you, that my joy might remain in you, and that your joy might be full.

When a deacon or a deacon's wife is living in carnality, their example brings harm to the church and weakens the influence of Christ in their community. Paul asks a pointed question in Romans 6:1. He asks, "What shall we say then? Shall we continue in sin, that grace may abound?" He answers his own question in Romans 6:2, by saying, "God forbid. How shall we, that are dead to sin, live any longer therein?"

Note Paul's remarks about the carnal members of the church in Rome, recorded in Romans 8:5-13:

> For they that are after the flesh do mind the things of the flesh; but they that are after the Spirit the things of the Spirit. For to be carnally minded is death; but to be spiritually minded is life and peace. Because the carnal mind is enmity against God: for it is not subject to the law of God, neither indeed can be. So then they that are in the flesh cannot please God. But ye are not in the flesh, but in the Spirit, if so be that the Spirit of God dwell in you. Now if any man have not the Spirit of

Christ, he is none of his. And if Christ be in you, the body is dead because of sin; but the Spirit is life because of righteousness. But if the Spirit of him that raised up Jesus from the dead dwell in you, he that raised up Christ from the dead shall also quicken your mortal bodies by his Spirit that dwelleth in you. Therefore, brethren, we are debtors, not to the flesh, to live after the flesh. For if ye live after the flesh, ye shall die: but if ye through the Spirit do mortify the deeds of the body, ye shall live.

The parable of the vine

It is God's will that every Christian live a Christlike life. Yet, there are many Christians who are struggling to live this life, not knowing where the necessary strength lies. Through the parable of the vine, Jesus illustrates that producing much fruit is the purpose for His followers. This parable also reveals where the followers of Christ are to find the strength to bear much fruit. They will find their strength in Him. Examine with me the parable of the vine, found in John 15:1-8.

I am the true vine, and my Father is the husbandman. Every branch in me that beareth not fruit he taketh away: and every branch that beareth fruit, he purgeth it, that it may bring forth more fruit. Now ye are clean through the word which I have spoken unto you. Abide in me, and I in you. As the branch cannot bear fruit of itself, except it abide in the vine; no more can ye, except ye abide in me. I am the vine, ye are the branches: He that abideth in me, and I in him, the same bringeth forth much fruit: for without me ye can do nothing. If a man abide not in me, he is cast forth as a branch, and is withered; and men gather them, and cast them into the fire, and they are burned. If ye abide in me, and my words abide in you, ye shall ask what ye will, and it shall be done unto you. Herein is my Father glorified, that ye bear much fruit; so shall ye be my disciples.

The word *parable* comes from the Greek word *parabello*. In the Greek, *para* means "beside," and *bello* means "to cast or throw." Jesus often used parables to illustrate a hidden truth. In doing so, He would draw a word picture. His word picture would share something familiar, cast alongside something unfamiliar to His hearers, to illustrate His truth. In the parable of the vine, Jesus drew His word picture around His hearer's familiarity with a vine in a vineyard. His hearers knew that a husbandman was the owner or caretaker of the vineyard and was responsible for its upkeep. They also knew the value the husbandman placed on the vine. The vine was chosen carefully to ensure it would be without disease and would support the grafted branches, producing much fruit. Jesus' audience knew that fruit came from the branches grafted into the vine. They also knew that the branches that did not graft into the vine died and were gathered and burned. It is on this backdrop that Jesus shares the parable of the vine.

By the use of this parable, Jesus would have His followers know that the world is God's vineyard, and God is the owner and caretaker of this world. Christ Himself is the "true vine" (John 15:1), carefully chosen by God (1 Pet. 1:20). His followers are the branches, and their purpose is to produce "much fruit" (John 15:5). This parable clearly illustrates that the only way a Christian can produce "much fruit" is by being grafted into Christ. Thus, the primary purpose for this parable is to inform the followers of Christ that they are to produce "much fruit," and Christ will provide them with the strength they will need to bear it.

There is a very important warning in this parable. Jesus says in John 15:2, "Every branch in me that beareth not fruit he taketh away . . ." In verse 6, Jesus adds, "If a man abide not in me, he is cast forth as a branch, and is withered: and men gather them, and cast them into the fire, and they are burned." Simply stated, those who pretend to be Christians, but are not, will be judged and cast into hell. In Matthew 7:15-23, Jesus further clarifies this fact. Even though He is speaking of the "false prophet," what He says is applicable to all who assume they are a Christian, but are not.

> Beware of false prophets, which come to you in sheep's clothing, but inwardly they are ravening wolves. Ye shall know them by their fruits. Do men gather grapes of thorns,

or figs of thistles? Even so every good tree bringeth forth good fruit; but a corrupt tree bringeth forth evil fruit. A good tree cannot bring forth evil fruit, neither can a corrupt tree bring forth good fruit. Every tree that bringeth not forth good fruit is hewn down, and cast into the fire. Wherefore by their fruits ye shall know them. Not everyone that saith unto me, Lord, Lord, shall enter into the kingdom of heaven; but he that doeth the will of my Father which is in heaven. Many will say to me in that day, Lord, Lord, have we not prophesied in thy name? and in thy name have cast out devils? and in thy name done many wonderful works? And then will I profess unto them, I never knew you: depart from me, ye that work iniquity.

Benefits of abiding in Christ

Before a deacon can accomplish God's will through his ministry, he must realize that his best efforts are not good enough. He needs a source of strength outside himself. He needs the Spirit of Christ to empower him. It is only when a believer is grafted into and abides in Christ that he is promised some wonderful benefits. In John 15:5, the believer is promised that his life will produce "much fruit." Note the progression Jesus reveals concerning fruit-bearing in this parable. In verse 2, we are told that unless one abides in the vine, there can be "no fruit," and the branch is ". . . taken away." The last part of verse 2, and continuing through verse 5, assures the

38

believer that if he continues to abide in Christ, his life will progress in fruit-bearing from "fruit," to "more fruit," to "much fruit."

Paul, in Galatians 5:22-23, reminds the follower of Christ that when he is walking in the Spirit his life will produce the fruit of the Spirit. He tells us, ". . . the fruit of the Spirit is love, joy, peace, longsuffering, gentleness, goodness, faith, meekness, temperance: against such there is no law." Paul adds in Ephesians 5:9, "For the fruit of the Spirit is in all goodness and righteousness and truth." When a deacon is walking in the Spirit, his life will reveal that same "goodness and righteousness and truth." He therefore will be a blessing to all who know him. His example will encourage others in the church to be more Christlike. What a benefit!

When a deacon is walking in the Spirit, he has the assurance that his prayers will be answered. Look at John 15:7: "If ye abide in me, and my words abide in you, ye shall ask what ye will, and it shall be done unto you." This is not a promise that says you can have anything you want, but rather a promise that if you are saved and Spirit-filled, your prayers will be answered because you will be focusing on God's will rather than your wants. I have never known a genuine Christian who did not desire to know more about the Lord and His will for their life.

To do the work of the deacon, spiritual wisdom is essential. Before Christ ascended back to heaven, He told His disciples He would send the Holy Spirit to provide them with the wisdom they would need to accomplish their spiritual responsibilities. In John

14:26, Jesus says, "But the Comforter, which is the Holy Ghost, whom the Father will send in my name, he shall teach you all things, and bring all things to your remembrance, whatsoever I have said unto you." It is God's will that a deacon possess spiritual wisdom. He must know God's Word and God's will to accomplish his responsibilities as a deacon. James 1:5 says, "If any of you lack wisdom, let him ask of God, that giveth to all men liberally, and upbraideth not; and it shall be given him." Do you long for spiritual wisdom?

When we allow un-confessed sin in our lives, we will be void of God's power. Isaiah 59:1-2, reminds us, "Behold, the LORD's hand is not shortened, that it cannot save; neither his ear heavy, that it cannot hear: But your iniquities have separated between you and your God, and your sins have hid his face from you, that he will not hear." Spiritual power is absent in the lives of many today who are a part of the church. As never before, the world needs to see the power of Christ made manifest through those who are associated with Him. It is only when a deacon is walking in the Spirit that he can experience the spiritual power necessary to accomplish God's will. In Acts 1:8, Christ shares with us, "But ye shall receive power, after that the Holy Ghost is come upon you . . ." Are you praying for God's power?

By walking in the Spirit, one can experience joy in serving Christ. How many church members do you know that demonstrate real Christian joy? The joy produced by the Spirit in the life of the believer is not pretentious, but real, pure, and satisfying. In

John 4:14, John likens the Spirit in the life of the believer to an artesian well, continuously supplying life's needs. He says, "But whosoever drinketh of the water that I shall give him shall never thirst; but the water that I shall give him shall be in him a well of water springing up into everlasting life." Are you a joyful Christian?

Another benefit of abiding in the Vine is that of living a purposeful life. In John 15:8, Jesus says, "Herein is my Father glorified, that ye bear much fruit . . ." Living as God requires not only glorifies God, but also benefits the individual Christian and the cause of Christ. Jeremiah 17:10 says, "I the LORD search the heart, I try the reins, even to give every man according to his ways, and according to the fruit of his doings." There is a difference between a *work* and the *fruit* one produces. While a *work* constitutes a single act, the *fruit* one produces contains seed that can reproduce more fruit, repeatedly. Thus, the fruit of the Christian will produce a purposeful life. Look over your shoulder; are you producing a purposeful life?

Every deacon should desire to be controlled by the Spirit

Every deacon should desire the Spirit of God to control his life because of what the Spirit does. When one is saved, the Spirit takes up residence in their life. Jesus says in John 14:16-17,"And I will pray the Father, and he shall give you another Comforter, that he may abide with you for ever; even the Spirit of truth; whom the world cannot receive, because it seeth him not, neither knoweth him: but ye know him; for he dwelleth with you, and shall be in you." Jesus shared these words with His disciples just prior to His return to heaven. His disciples' hearts were broken. They knew He was soon to leave them. They had envisioned Jesus setting up His kingdom on earth and including them in His kingdom's leadership. He knew their sorrow and their need for comfort. He promised them, and His followers to come, that the Holy Spirit would come as a Comforter and establish His dwelling in the heart of those who would give their life to Him. The Spirit would be "the Spirit of truth," and His Spirit would dwell within their hearts forever, neither to leave nor forsake them.

The Holy Spirit gives the believer the assurance of their salvation. Every Christian doubts his salvation from time to time. In Luke 7:19, we read that John the Baptist had his doubts. "And John calling unto him two of his disciples sent them to Jesus, saying, Art thou he that should come? or look we for another?" When Satan tries to deceive us, we need to remember what Paul says in Romans 8:16-17, "The Spirit itself beareth witness with our spirit, that we are the children of God: And if children, then heirs; heirs of God, and joint-heirs with Christ; if so be that we suffer with him, that we may be also glorified together." When we have reached the bottom of the barrel, and it seems no one cares, the Holy Spirit has a special way of assuring us that all is well. He reminds us that we belong to Jesus!

The indwelling of the Spirit in the life of the believer is God's pledge to pay the believer's price for redemption in full. In Ephesians 1:13-14, we read:

> In whom ye also trusted, after that ye heard the word of truth, the gospel of your salvation: in whom also after that ye believed, ye were sealed with that holy Spirit of promise, which is the earnest of our inheritance until the redemption of the purchased possession, unto the praise of his glory.

The word *earnest* means "something of value given by a buyer to a seller to bind a bargain" (*Merriam-Webster's Collegiate Dictionary*, 10th ed.). The word *earnest* in Ephesians 1:13-14 reminds us that the price for redemption has been paid in full. God's gift of the Spirit in the life of the believer is God's pledge that assures our salvation.

Another benefit of the Holy Spirit is that He reveals to us our sins. Jesus says in John 16:8, "And when he is come, he will reprove the world of sin . . ." I do not know of anyone who enjoys having his or her sins revealed. However, the Spirit reveals our sins to us, not for enjoyment, but that we might address them and benefit from the process.

The Holy Spirit gives the believer the power to share his witness to others. Luke says in Acts 1:8, "But ye shall receive power, after that the Holy Ghost is come upon you: and ye shall be witnesses unto me both in Jerusalem, and in all Judea, and in Samaria, and unto the uttermost part of the earth." One has but to read the book of Acts to know that the leaders who significantly influenced the Christian movement in the first century were those who were filled with the Holy Spirit. Today, the average Southern Baptist church baptizes less than ten new converts per year. There is a real need for individual Christians to submit themselves to the Holy Spirit's control, allowing His power to help them be the witness they should be. As a deacon in your church, are you sharing your faith with the lost in your community? Are you setting the example for witnessing?

Some deacons are of the opinion that witnessing is just too difficult. They excuse themselves by saying, "I don't know how to witness!" or "I am afraid to share my faith!" Paul tells us how we can overcome the overwhelming aspects of witnessing.

> For they that are after the flesh do mind the things of the flesh; but they that are after the Spirit the things of the Spirit. For to be carnally minded is death; but to be spiritually minded is life and peace. Because the carnal mind is enmity against God: for it is not subject to the law of God, neither indeed can be. So then they that are in the flesh cannot please God. But ye are not in the flesh, but in the Spirit, if so be that the Spirit of God dwell in you. Now if any man have not the Spirit of Christ, he is none of his. And if Christ be in you, the body is dead because of sin; but the Spirit is life because of righteousness. But if the Spirit of him that raised up Jesus from the dead dwell in you, he that raised up Christ

from the dead shall also quicken your mortal bodies by his Spirit that dwelleth in you. Therefore, brethren, we are debtors, not to the flesh, to live after the flesh. For if ye live after the flesh, ye shall die: but if ye through the Spirit do mortify the deeds of the body, ye shall live. For as many are led by the Spirit of God, they are the sons of God.

—Romans 8:5-14

If we think that it is difficult to witness in our community, consider how difficult it was for those in the city of Rome to share their faith during the days of Paul. The church at Rome was located in one of the most pagan cities the world has ever known. This church had no buildings, no trained leadership, no literature, no Bibles, and the members of the church were extremely poor. Yet, the members of the church at Rome were given a mandate to win their city to Christ. In their despondency to do so, Paul, under the leadership of the Holy Spirit, sought to encourage them. He reminded them of three simple truths. First, he reminded them they were *dead to self.*

The word *self* refers to the old sin nature—to that old nature that opposes God—that is associated with whatever is weak and ungodly. Paul tells them, "That old 'you' is dead." It is important for the Christian to understand this, for self cannot do the work of God and is not expected to do the work of God. Paul tells them ". . . they that are in the flesh cannot please God" (Rom. 8:8). Paul has come to this realization when he says, ". . . I know that in me (that is, in my flesh,) dwelleth no good thing . . ." (Rom. 7:18). Paul acknowledges what many have failed to recognize—"I can't"—but—"I can do all things through Christ which strengtheneth me" (Phil. 4:13). Jesus reminds us of this truth as He challenges His disciples to follow him. ". . . If any man will come after me, let him deny himself . . ." (Matt. 16:24). In all that we do for Christ, we need to learn that it is not what we can do, but what Christ can do through us, for we are dead!

Second, Paul reminds the church at Rome that *they were alive in Christ!* In Romans 6:11, Paul says, "Likewise reckon ye also yourselves to be dead indeed unto sin, but alive unto God through Jesus Christ our Lord." Why is it important for a Christian to know they are alive in Christ? Because when Christ came to live in our hearts, He brought with Him all that He is. As Christians, we have the fullness of the Godhead dwelling within us, for ". . . greater is he that is in you, than he that is in the world" (1 John 4:4). Paul tells us in Galatians 2:20, "I am crucified with Christ: nevertheless, I live; yet not I, but Christ liveth in me . . ." We are also told by Paul in 2 Corinthians 5:17, ". . . if any man be in Christ, he is a new creature: old things have passed away; behold all things are become new." Knowing that we are alive in Christ gives new meaning to Acts 1:8: "But ye shall receive power, after that the Holy Ghost is come upon you: and ye shall be witnesses unto me both in Jerusalem, and in all Judea, and in Samaria, and unto the uttermost part of the earth." Knowing that Christ lives within us gives us courage and strength to witness to others.

The third thing Paul shares with the church at Rome was that *Christians are responsible to God for others*. Paul tells us we are debtors to share with whomever God places in our life. However, the ultimate One to whom we are responsible to for sharing our faith is God. We are to surrender ourselves to witness for Him, allowing Him to use us as He sees fit, remembering, we are dead to self, we are alive in Christ, and we are responsible to Him for others.

God commands we be filled with the Spirit

Paul shares God's command to us in Ephesians 5:18: "And be not drunk with wine, wherein is excess; but be filled with the Spirit." In Greek grammar, the phrase "be filled" is an imperative, carrying with it the idea that you must be filled. To "be filled" is in the present tense, which signifies continuous motion. It means, "Go on being filled." "Be filled" is plural. Thus, the filling of the Spirit is not just for the few, but for all Christians. To "be filled" is in the passive voice, which means the subject and the verb are not active, but rather acted upon. You do not become filled with the Spirit by more activity, but rather one is filled with the Spirit when he meets the requirements to be filled.

What are the requirements to be filled with the Spirit? Before I answer this question, permit me to clarify what I mean by being "filled" with the Spirit. I believe, through the act of conversion, one receives all of the Holy Spirit he/she will ever receive. The gift of the Spirit occurs at the moment of conversion. Yet, the Holy Spirit does not have total possession of the new Christian at conversion. In the parable of the vine, we noted a progression in the production of fruit from the Christian, from "fruit" to "much fruit." We also noted where Paul said that although the carnal person is saved, his life demonstrates that the Spirit does not control him (Rom. 8:7). I believe the Christian has a choice to be filled with the Spirit.

In order to be filled with the Spirit, the believer's first requirement is the choice to be filled with the Spirit. The Spirit will not force Himself upon the believer. Jesus says in Matthew 5:6, "Blessed are they which do hunger and thirst after righteousness: for they shall be filled." Every Christian should desire to be filled with the Spirit, for in being filled they will be indwelt with all the fullness of the Godhead. In the parable of the vine, Jesus reminds His followers, ". . . without me, ye can do nothing" (John 15:5). When you consider who the Spirit is and what He can do in the Christian's life, choosing to permit Him to control your life should be easy.

The believer's second requirement to be filled with the Spirit is to deal with any sin in his life. In that Christ sent the Spirit to live in the believer, to convict of sin (John 16:8), and as a Comforter (John 15:26), there can be no comfort for the believer who has un-confessed sin in his life. The deacon's relation to Christ is the foundation for his ministry. He must be right with Christ. This means he must be saved and Spirit-filled, if he is to accomplish what God would have him accomplish.

Third, if a Christian is to be filled with the Spirit, they are required to ask God to be filled with His Spirit. By asking for the Spirit, the believer acknowledges his inability to accomplish God's will without the Spirit's help. By asking to be filled with the Spirit, a Christian evidences his willingness to humble himself and become submissive to the Spirit's leadership. God will not force His Spirit upon us, nor will He give us what we do not want or will not use. We must ask God for the infilling of His Spirit.

In light of what I have shared in this chapter, let me ask you again about your relation to Christ. Does your life demonstrate that you have been saved? A lost or carnal person has no real desire to spend time in Bible study, prayer, or soul winning. Neither is the lost or carnal person faithful to the church's worship services, nor in the financial support of his church. One who is saved demonstrates a life that has moved from un-commitment to commitment concerning the things of God. If you are saved, but the Spirit does not control you, you are carnal. The flesh controls the carnal person. In Matthew 7:20, Jesus tells us how we can know the commitment level of a Christian. He said, ". . . by their fruits ye shall know them." Are you bearing "much fruit"?

If you are lost or have doubts about your relation to Christ, you need to settle this issue. You cannot serve Christ as a deacon if you are not saved or if you live in a constant state of doubt about your salvation experience. In the flyleaf of my Bible is a prayer, which I often use in witnessing. If you are lost or if you are in doubt about your salvation, I want to encourage you to pray this prayer. Will you pray with me now?

Dear Lord,

I come to You, acknowledging that You are the Christ, the Son of the living God. You came to earth. You were born of a virgin. You lived a sinless life. You died my death and paid my sin debt in full at the cross. You were buried and arose again on the third day.

I acknowledge it was for my sin that You went to the cross. I confess that I am a sinner and say with a broken heart, "Forgive me of all my sins." Come into my heart, and save me for Christ's sake.

In Jesus' name,
Amen

If you prayed this prayer, and you now are assured of your salvation, you need to share your decision with your family, your pastor, and your church. You also should be baptized, for this is the first act of obedience for the Christian (Acts 2:38).

If you are saved, does the Spirit control your life? The same fear that prevents many who are lost from coming to Christ also prevents Christians from giving themselves more fully to Christ once they are saved. Solomon says, in Proverbs 29:25, "The fear of man bringeth a snare: but whoso putteth his trust in the

LORD shall be safe." If there is some un-confessed sin in your life that is preventing you from being all you could be for Christ, will you pray this prayer?

Dear Lord,

I acknowledge my sins (name the sin or sins) and my failure to be all I could be (and should be) as your child, as a mate, as a parent, as a church member, and as a deacon.

Please forgive me and enable me to be pleasing in Your sight. Give me both an understanding of what You would have me do and the empowering of Your Spirit to accomplish what needs to be done.

In Jesus' name,
Amen

If you prayed this prayer and you have rededicated yourself to Christ, let me challenge you to share your decision with your wife and family. Go forward in your church this coming Sunday morning during the invitation and acknowledge your decision to your pastor and the church. You may wish to challenge church members to evaluate their relationship with Christ, and if need be, join you at the altar to rededicate themselves to Christ. Your willingness to be used by God could be the means of starting a revival in your church.

Chapter 2

The Deacon in Relation to His Family

What is your spiritual relation to your family? If a deacon does not have a good relationship with his family, he is not right with Christ, nor can he be right with the church. A mountain of evidence today reveals that marriages are in serious trouble. God designed marriages to be anchored upon Christ and His Word. Satan, therefore, will do all he can to prevent this from happening. Satan's attacks against marriages are focused on "Formation," "Foundation," and "Fulfillment."

Consider Satan's attack against marriage at "Formation." Long before a couple approaches the marriage altar, Satan is at work to destroy their marriage. His attacks against the couple began when they were born. He works hard to prevent parents from raising their children in the Word of God and leading them to experience a personal relationship with Christ. Since 90 percent of the youth in America do not attend church and 60 percent of the youth raised in church drop out in their teen years, you must conclude that Satan is successful in his attacks against the home. Satan knows that it is impossible for a couple to give their best self to their mate in marriage if they have not given themselves first to Christ before marriage. The couple who approaches the marriage altar without Christ is also without the indwelling Spirit of Christ. Therefore, their life is void of the Spirit's truth, power, guidance, comfort, and teaching. A marriage established on a faulty foundation will fail without divine intervention.

Once a marriage has occurred, Satan begins to attack at its "Foundation." To have a spiritual marriage, a couple must know Christ as their Savior and anchor their home upon God's Word and His will. Preventing a couple from accomplishing a spiritual marriage is paramount to Satan. He will preoccupy a couple, causing them to place their focus on finding a job that pays more money, securing a bigger home, or involving their children in recreational activities. He will do whatever it takes to prevent a couple from establishing their marriage on the principles of God's Word. As time passes and the children grow older, Satan knows the children of a marriage not anchored on Christ and His Word will have difficulty building their own marriage on a sure foundation.

Satan's attacks against marriage and the home are subtle. He lurks in the shadows, masterfully applying pressure as needed to disrupt or destroy. His ultimate goal against a marriage is at the point of

"Fulfillment." When Satan can prevent a couple from accomplishing God's purpose for their marriage, he has obtained ultimate victory over their marriage.

What is God's will for your marriage?

When I ask couples in the marriage retreat I conduct if their marriage is successful, most will answer, "Yes!" However, their answer often is predicated upon material gain, rather than on their accomplishments of God's will. For a marriage to fulfill God's purpose, the couple must know Christ as their Savior. They must make His will for their lives a priority, and they must strive daily to bring God's will to fruition. To obtain fulfillment in marriage, a couple must know where they are going and be willing to trust Christ to get them there. Too many couples today are going nowhere, hoping to arrive somewhere.

When I was fourteen years old, I accepted Christ as my Savior at the West Anniston Baptist Church, in Anniston, Alabama. One night, two weeks after my conversion, as I was laying in an old iron swing on my grandmother's front porch, the Lord called me to preach. As a new Christian and a young boy, I had my doubts about what God was doing in my life. When I was in my early twenties, I went to the woods one morning under the pretense of going hunting. When I arrived at the place where I was to hunt, I left my rifle in the truck, walked into the woods, and sat down next to a big oak tree. Over the next few hours, I poured my heart out to God; and as I left the woods that morning, God's call upon my life was settled.

God calls the butcher, the baker, and the candle-stick-maker. He has a specific purpose and plan for every life. The closer we live to the design God has for our lives, the more blessed we are, and the better example we will be for His glory.

Once in a marriage retreat I was conducting, a woman approached me and said, "Brother Don, you said, 'God has a plan for every life and every marriage.' I have never thought that I or my marriage was that important to God." I answered her by saying, "You are important to God and so is your marriage. Have you ever thought about how many people your life affects? You are the only Christian example some people have. They watch how you live as an individual. They also observe your actions and reactions with your mate. Both you and your marriage are very important to God."

How can you know God's will?

James 1:5 tells us, "If any of you lack wisdom, let him ask of God, that giveth to all men liberally, and upbraideth not; and it shall be given him." In 1 John 3:22 we read, "And whatsoever we ask, we receive of him, because we keep his commandments, and do those things that are pleasing in his sight." These two verses reveal that one can know the will of God by asking God for His will and doing what God requires.

Solomon says in Proverbs 16:3, "Commit thy works unto the LORD, and thy thoughts shall be established." In other words, you do not think right to do right; rather you do right to think right. When you begin to implement the following fifteen principles on a daily basis, you are well on your way to understanding the will of God for your life.

1. You give your heart and life to Christ.

To know God's will for your life, you must know God. In John 3:3 we read, ". . . Except a man be born again, he cannot see the kingdom of God." This verse carries two significant meanings. First, it reveals that if one is to understand God's plan and purpose for their life, then they must first give themselves to Christ. This is done by acknowledging themselves a sinner, separated from God by virtue of their sin, and void of His presence and power. In such a state, one cannot visualize God's desires for their life or what He could do through their life. They are lost! They are without Christ, His forgiveness, and the empowering of His Spirit. They must acknowledge their sinful state, confess their sin, and ask Christ for His forgiveness. Second, this verse reveals that when a person accepts Christ into their life, their spiritual eyes will be opened, enabling them to visualize God's plan and purpose for their life.

2. You do not grieve the Spirit nor quench the Spirit, but rather you walk in the Spirit.

It bothers me when I hear someone refer to the Holy Spirit as an "It." The Spirit is a part of the Godhead, (God the Father, God the Son, and God the Holy Spirit). The Spirit, like the Father and the Son, can be neglected, offended, and denied. How we treat the Spirit of God speaks volumes of who we are in relation to Christ. If we love and respect Christ, if we understand the value of His Spirit, we will desire the Spirit to control our life. We should give ourselves to Him in total abandonment. We will not grieve Him by our actions and words. Paul challenges us in Ephesians 4:30: "And grieve not the holy Spirit of God . . ." In 1 Thessalonians 5:19, Paul would have us know we are not to quench the Spirit. As Christians, our desire should be to ". . . Walk in the Spirit" (Gal. 5:16). If you want to know God's will, examine your relationship with the Spirit of God. Asking Him to take control of your life, while treating Him with resentment, is not practical.

3. You pray without ceasing.

Someone asked me recently how much time I devoted to prayer each day. I could not give them a definitive answer. I have never put a stopwatch on my time in prayer. I begin each day with prayer, and I pray all through the day. There is a stain on the carpet beside our bed from the oil from my forehead, which has been left over the years as I have knelt and closed the day with prayer. Paul tells us in 1 Thessalonians 5:17 that we are to "Pray without ceasing." How much time do you spend in prayer each day? For whom and for what do you pray?

Prayer is such a vital part of the live of the believer. It is imperative that we speak to God about the events of our lives. We need His input! We need His wisdom and guidance. We need His mercy and grace. It is through prayer that our relationship with God is enriched, our relationship with Christ is assured, and our relationship with the Spirit is strengthened. It is through prayer we can better understand God's will for our lives.

4.   You study to show yourself approved.

For the deacon to know God's will for his life, he must study God's Word. Paul says in 2 Timothy 2:15, "Study to show thyself approved unto God, a workman that needeth not to be ashamed, rightly dividing the word of truth." Note this verse. First, we see the challenge. The Christian is to study the Bible. Second, we are told why—we are workmen. A workman needs guidelines and instructions to accomplish his job. David says in Psalms 119:103-105, "How sweet are thy words unto my taste! yea, sweeter than honey to my mouth! Through thy precepts I get understanding: therefore I hate every false way. Thy word is a lamp unto my feet, and a light unto my path."

Knowing God's Word and doing God's will are two different things. Paul reminds us in this verse that the Christian, as a workman, must study God's Word and implement God's will by "rightly dividing the word of truth" in his daily life. When this is done, the deacon will not have to be ashamed of what he is doing for Christ.

5.   You attend church regularly.

Do you and your family attend worship services at your church regularly? In the four churches that I pastored, with rare exception, the deacons and their families were present for each of the worship services. Deacons are to lead by example! How can you expect others in the church to be faithful to the worship services if you and your family are not faithful?

Paul tells us in Hebrews 10:25, "Not forsaking the assembling of ourselves together, as the manner of some is; but exhorting one another: and so much the more, as ye see the day approaching." Church attendance is vital for the believer's development and growth. It is through the church most come to know Christ as Savior. Church attendance provides the believer with biblical teachings, encouragement for times of discouragement, and support and guidance in times of weakness. Every deacon and his family should love and support the church and be faithful to its services.

6. You train your children in the way they should go.

Most parents are committed to educating their children. Twelve long years they enforce rules and regulations on their children, assisting them every way they know how to ensure they graduate from high school. During these days, parents also train their children in social conduct, teaching them how they are to deal with others. They give guidance to their children for their life's occupation. Yet, most parents today give little or no instructions to their child's spiritual development. Solomon says in Proverbs 22:6: "Train up a child in the way he should go . . ." If a child is to be trained in biblical principles, it must be done primarily through the example of their parents.

Permit me to share with you one of the things I told each of our two sons a few days before they were married. I said, "I want to challenge you to be the best Christian man you can be, the best husband, father, friend, and neighbor. I want you to think about any strengths and weaknesses in these areas you observed in my life. My reason for asking you to do this is to challenge you to be a better man than I have been." There comes a day in every parent's life when their children will leave home. What their children do and what they become in life will be a reflection of how they were raised. As you raise your children, I want to challenge you to remember Paul's remarks: "And ye fathers, provoke not your children to wrath: but bring them up in the nurture and admonition of the Lord" (Eph. 6:4). Be that example God would have you be!

7. Husbands, love your wives.

In a marriage, one's relationship with God is predicated upon their relationship with their mate. If you are not right with your mate, you are not right with God. Peter reminds the husband that he and his wife are ". . . heirs together of the grace of life . . ." (1 Pet. 3:7). If you truly desire to know God's will for your life, ensure that your relationship with you mate is all God would have it be. A married couple cannot live independent of one another. What one does affects them both. Therefore, love your mate! Do all you can to help your mate fulfill God's call on them. Love is reciprocal! The more love you give your mate, the more love you will receive in return.

8. Wives, submit yourself unto your own husband.

Selfishness will never lead one to finding God's will. A wife's relationship to her husband is as important as his relationship is to her. For a wife to accomplish God's will for her life, she must accept God's teachings about her role within the home. If she is unwilling to submit herself to the biblical truths concerning her relationship to her husband, then she is unwilling to do God's will. In Ephesians 5:22, Paul tells the wife, "Wives, submit yourselves unto your own husbands, as unto the Lord." Paul's instructions are not to demean a wife. He is not placing the wife in a degrading role, implying the husband is of more value than she is.

In today's world, feminism has distorted the truth about women. God's Word does not place men on a pedestal calling for women to bow to their husband's every wish. To the contrary, the Bible places women in a very special role. Listen to what Peter says about how the husband is to honor his wife: "Likewise, ye husbands dwell with them [your wife] according to knowledge, giving honor unto the wife, as unto the weaker vessel . . ." (1 Pet. 3:7). The Bible however, does require that the wife submit herself unto her husband, for he is the spiritual leader in the home.

As a deacon's wife, what would you say about your relationship with your husband? Do you know God's will for your life in your marriage? Are you a submissive wife? Are you helping your husband to be the spiritual leader within your home?

9. You love your neighbor as yourself.

When I was a boy, we knew everyone who lived in our community. Most of the dads worked at the local foundry and most of the moms stayed at home. All the children played together and went to school and church together. However, in today's world, most people do not know who lives next door to them.

Over the years, Linda and I have moved on several occasions. Each time we have moved, after we had settled in, I would visit each of our neighbors and introduce myself to them. I would tell them, "I am Don Ledbetter. My wife, Linda, and our two sons, Steve and Stan, are the ones who just moved into your community. I have come by today just to let you know who we are. I also want to tell you we are a Christian family. As such, we want to be a good neighbor. I won't be knocking down your door bothering you, but I do want to make myself available to you as a friend. If I can help you or your family in any way, I am available. If you need to borrow my tools or truck, give me a call. If you have any spiritual needs I can assist you with, or if there is anything you would like for me to pray with you about, give me a call." Each Christmas, Linda and I buy a Christmas gift for each of the four families that live closest to us in our subdivision. It is amazing how many doors have opened to share Christ with neighbors over the years.

God's will often is revealed to us when we are involved in doing what we know a Christian should do. Do you know who lives next door to you? As a deacon, what are you and your wife doing to share Christ with your neighbors? Paul reminds us in Romans 13:9, "... Thou shalt love thy neighbor as thyself."

10. You seek first the kingdom of God.

Seeking the kingdom of God involves knowing God's will for your life. What importance do you place upon knowing God's will? The excuse many have today for not doing what they should do is, "I don't have time." I have discovered that people make time for what they really want to do. It would do us well to remember that our life is framed in time. We only have a certain number of days to live; therefore, we must be good stewards of our days.

In Psalm 39:4, David says, "Lord, make me to know mine end, and the measure of my days, what it is: that I may know how frail I am." David is not asking God to tell him when he is going to die or where or how. David is asking God to help him come to grips with the fact that he is going to die. Most of us are reluctant to think about our death. Yet, the Bible tells us that death for all of us is an appointed event (Heb. 9:27). Look at David's second request in this verse of Scripture. "Lord, make me to know the measure of my day." David is not asking God to inform him what he will accomplish in his life. David is asking God to help him understand the difference between what he is doing with his life and what he could be doing with his life with God's help. David closes this verse with a plea for God to remember that he is dependent upon Him to accomplish anything worthwhile.

The success of the ministry of the deacon rests upon his desire to place Christ and His kingdom's work at the focal point of his life. In the Sermon on the Mount, Jesus tells us not to be overly concerned with the things of life: "But seek ye first the kingdom of God . . ." (Matt. 6:33).

11. You love the Lord with all your heart.

Love is more than an emotion! Love is an action! Paul reminds us that what we do through our body is under our control. "But I keep under my body, and bring it into subjection . . ." (1 Cor. 9:27). Yet, the outward actions of the body are controlled by the "inner man." Jesus says in Luke 6:45, "A good man out of the good treasure of his heart bringeth forth that which is good; and an evil man out of the evil treasure of his heart bringeth forth that which is evil: for of the abundance of the heart his mouth speaketh." In order to love God with all your heart, you must have Christ in your heart.

It should be remembered that if you revert to a carnal state, your love for God and the things of God will not be as it should be. The best way to discover your spiritual condition is to examine what you are doing for Christ. Jesus, speaking of the Christian's commitment, says in Matthew 7:20, "Wherefore by their fruits ye shall known them." What do your works say about your love for Christ? Moses says, in Deuteronomy 13:3, ". . . For the LORD your God proveth you, to know whether ye love the LORD your God with all your heart and with all your soul."

12. You confess your faults to and pray for one another.

When the boys were young, the role of praying for our evening meal rotated. One evening I would pray, the next evening Linda would pray, then Steve, then Stan. The boys often prayed the prayer, "I bow my head and fold my hands and thank the Lord for this good bread, Amen." In an attempt to encourage the boys to make their prayers more personal, I stopped Stan one evening and asked him to pray "out of his heart." He tried to get his brother to pray, but it was his turn. I told him we would wait on him until he could think of what he wanted to say. We waited and waited. Finally, he said, "Lord, I want to thank you for my sins! I enjoy them! Amen."

Unlike a child, a mature Christian often has difficulty confessing their sins. Yet, God requires that we confess our sins. Lister to what James says about this in James 5:16: "Confess your faults one to another, and pray one for another, that ye may be healed . . ." James tells the Christian they are to acknowledge their sinful actions toward their neighbor and should do so by telling their neighbor they are sorry for the wrong they have done to them. He also alludes to the fact that some sickness may result from how they have treated their neighbor. The truth implied is, if you want to know God's will for your life, you must be obedient to God's requirements for your daily living. If you are not going to do what God requires of you, why seek His will for your life? We should remember what David says in Psalm 32:5: "I acknowledge my sin unto thee, and mine iniquity have I not hid. I said, I will confess my transgressions unto the Lord; and thou forgavest the iniquity of my sin." We should confess our sinful deeds not only to the neighbor we have offended, but also to God.

Praying for others is beneficial to our spiritual growth. In Matthew 5:44, Jesus says, ". . . Love your enemies, bless them that curse you, do good to them that hate you, and pray for them which despitefully use you, and persecute you." Praying for others gives us a better perspective on who they are and what they need. Our prayers for them make us mindful that we too are not perfect and that we stand in need of God's grace and blessings. In short, praying for others makes us more aware of our own shortcomings and our dependency upon the Lord.

13. You give and it shall be given unto you.

I have never met a stingy Christian that was worth their spiritual salt! God so loved, He gave (John 3:16). God has not called the Christian to be a sponge, absorbing all the goodness he can obtain. The Christian is a vessel designed to be filled to over-flowing. In Luke 6:38, we read, "Give, and it shall be given unto you; good measure, pressed down, and shaken together, and running over, shall men give into your bosom. For with the same measure that ye mete withal it shall be measured to you again." The best measure of a man's commitment to Christ is his giving. What does your giving say about you?

When the Christian absorbs what he receives from God and does not share it with others, he becomes stagnate. The blessings stop! Again this illustrates the importance of seeking to know God's will. God will not give you what you will not use! What are you doing with the things God has given to you? What about your tithe? Your talent? Your spiritual gifts? Your time?

14. You do all as unto the Lord.

How should a Christian live his life? Is he justified by not giving his best on his job if his employer is unjust? Does he have the right to treat his family in an unkind manner when they do not do everything for him that he thinks they should? How is a Christian to live before his friends? If they drink, should he? If they curse, should he? Paul says, "And whatsoever ye do in word or deed, do all in the name of the Lord Jesus, giving thanks to God and the Father by him" (Col. 3:17). Paul says that what you do with and for others should be done as if you were doing it for the Lord. Jesus illustrates this truth in Matthew 25:37-40: ". . . when saw we thee an hungred, and fed thee? or thirsty, and gave thee drink? When saw we thee a stranger, and took thee in? or naked, and clothed thee? Or when saw we thee sick, or in prison, and came unto thee? And the King shall answer and say unto them, Verily I say unto you, Inasmuch as ye have done it unto one of the least of these my brethren, ye have done it unto me."

To know God's will involves living out the Christian life day by day. Is this not the way it is in every other aspect of our life? If we want to play an instrument, we must have a true desire to do so. We associate with those who can help us learn how to play our instrument. We spend time with them learning what they can teach us. We absorb all we can and share with others all we have learned.

What is of most value to us, in knowing God's will, is a desire to be more equipped to serve Him. We should not seek to know His will for the sole purpose of knowing, but for implementing His will in order to help advance His kingdom and honor His Name.

15. You give thanks in everything.

Praise is an important part of the Christian's life. David tells us that God inhabits the praise of his people (Ps. 22:3). Paul tells us, "In every thing give thanks: for this is the will of God in Christ Jesus concerning you" (1 Thess. 5:18). Praising God "in everything" is not an easy task. If we said we did this well, most of us would have to ask God to forgive us for being dishonest. However, praise is important for several reasons. First, one's praise for God's goodness reveals why they are grateful. Their praise provides a clear description of what they believe is worthy of praise and helps the individual to examine his priorities. Second, one's praise serves as a witness to others, revealing what the individual Christian believes is important in his life. As God reveals His will for your life, give Him praise! The best way to praise Him is by doing what you know God would have you do.

How does Satan prevent you from doing God's will?

Take a moment and consider all the "wants" Satan uses to attack the home in America today. When a young couple is first married, they want a home. Then they want to furnish their home. They want a better car or another car, because they both work. As their incomes increase, he wants a boat. He has to have a truck to pull the boat, so he wants a truck. She wants more clothes. After all, she works and she needs to look her best. What are nice clothes without the accessories? She wants a bigger ring. When the children arrive, the house they first bought becomes too small, so they want a bigger house. They want their children's life to be better than their life was when they were children, so they want more and better things for their children.

The average American goes though life always wanting. There is nothing wrong with wanting or having things. The problem comes when wanting and having controls you. When was the last time you paused and thanked God for what you have? Most often, we do not appreciate what we have until we do not have it anymore. Satan causes many to focus on wanting the wrong things. Jesus asks, in Mark 8:36-37, "For what shall it profit a man, if he shall gain the whole world, and lose his own soul? Or what shall a man give in exchange for his soul?" The things Satan offers are temporary. What Christ offers is eternal. It is Christ's desire that we base our "wants" on His Word and His will for our lives. In so doing, we will be blessed and He will be glorified.

Consider all the activities that Satan bombards the home with today. Many homes are in chaos, with parents running up and down the road, carrying their children from one event to another. In most marriages, both parents work outside the home. Their children are involved in school and with school events. Many children are involved in karate classes, dancing lessons, baseball, football, soccer, basketball, tennis, piano lessons, guitar lessons, voice lessons, fishing and hunting, homework, dating, parties, etc.

With all the activities of the average home today, who has time for church? This is exactly why Satan keeps families busy doing things. What is Satan's strategy? His objective is to keep a family preoccupied. His ploy is deceptive. He knows if he can keep a family busy in activities that bring momentary pleasure, he can prevent them from focusing on doing things that will advance the kingdom of God. Given their proper place and time, there is nothing wrong with activities. The problem arises when momentary pleasures prevent a couple from serving Christ as they should.

Confusion over the role of the mates in marriage is another way Satan seeks to prevent couples from accomplishing the will of God. Some years ago, at the Southern Baptist Convention, a pastor came to the microphone to share a motion. His motion stated that what Paul says about the wife being submissive to her husband in Ephesians 5 has no relevance for our present society. His motion received no creditable attention, nor should it have, for the Bible teaches that the husband is the spiritual leader in the home. Paul says in Ephesians 5:23, "For the husband is the head of the wife, even as Christ is the head of the church . . ." As the spiritual leader in his home, Paul shares how the husband is to treat his wife in Ephesians 5:25. He says, "Husbands, love your wives, even as Christ also loved the church, and gave himself for it." In 1 Peter 3:7, Peter says, "Likewise, ye husbands, dwell with them according to knowledge, giving honour unto the wife, as unto the weaker vessel, and as being heirs together of the grace of life; that your prayers be not hindered."

Satan also uses disrespectful and ungrateful children to prevent families from accomplishing God's will. A man approached me one night after a revival service and asked me to pray for his son. When I asked what he wanted me to pray about concerning his son, he said, "I can't get him to do anything. He will not clean up his room. He does not do his homework. He won't come to church." I said, "How old is your son?" He said, "He is fourteen years old." Then he said, "I have a real problem with him; he just won't mind me." I said, "Sir, I don't mean to be disrespectful, but you don't have a problem with your son. Your son has a problem with you! You are the father of this boy and you have the responsibility of raising him. He lives in your home, eats the food you provide, and wears the clothes you provide. He should have enough respect for you and his mother to be obedient. He has learned over the years what you and his mother will permit him to do. If he lived in my house, he would abide by my rules, or else. If he got so big that I could not discipline him while he was awake, God help him when he went to sleep." (We both laughed.) This man assured me he was going home to change the way he was raising his son.

Some parents allow their children to do as they please, because the grown-ups are unwilling to deal with their wrath or rebellion. Parents have an obligation in the raising of their children to do their best to help them be all they can be. Parents are to be a living demonstration of God's will before their children, showing them the benefits of trusting God. Children need godly parents if this is to be accomplished. Godly parents consist of a man and a woman, saved by God's grace, who know God's will, are in God's place of service striving to accomplish His Will, and who treat their children as gifts from God, over whom they are stewards. Are you and your mate godly parents?

It is difficult for a couple to know or do God's will when they are constantly arguing with one another. One of Satan's most productive means of creating marital conflict is through a couple's sexual relationship. When God created Adam and Eve and commanded them, ". . . Be fruitful and multiply . . ." (Gen. 1.28), He ". . . saw every thing that he had made, and, behold, it was very good . . ." (Gen. 1:31). Thus, Adam and Eve were created to enjoy a physical relationship through which they could propagate their lineage. Sex, however, is more than a means to reproduce. In the bonds of marriage, sex is the climax of love.

What about your sexual relationship with your mate? This is a subject many couples are reluctant to talk about; however, the sale of pornography is at an all-time high. Paul reminds the husband and wife: "Let the husband render unto the wife due benevolence: and likewise also the wife unto the husband. The wife hath not power of her own body, but the husband: and likewise also the husband hath not power of his own body, but the wife. Defraud ye not one the other, except it be with consent for a time, that ye may give yourselves to fasting and prayer; and come together again, that Satan tempt you not for your incontinency" (1 Cor. 7:3-5). Paul is warning married couples to remember that their sexual relationship is so important to marital harmony they cannot afford to allow Satan to affect it.

A deacon's home should be a Christ-centered home

Some people teach that a Christ-centered home is a home of perfection. There is no such place! My secretary came into my office one morning and said, "There is a distraught woman here who wants to talk to you about a marital problem." When the person came into my office, it was obvious she was upset about something. When I asked her what she wanted to share with me, she said, "My husband and I had an argument last night." I waited for her to finish her story, but she just sat and looked at me. After a few moments, I said, "Are you upset because you and your husband argued, or are you upset because of what you argued about?" With a strange look on her face and with a defiant voice, she responded, "Brother Don, you know Christians don't argue!" When I asked her who told her Christians never argue, she just looked at me. When I shared with her that she was wrong and Christians do argue from time to time, she thought I was being condescending.

A Christ-centered home is not a home where Christians always do everything just as Christ would have them do it. John reminds us in 1 John 1:8, "If we say that we have no sin, we deceive ourselves, and the truth is not in us." Paul says in Romans 3:10, ". . . There is none righteous, no not one." In Romans 3:23, Paul adds, "For all have sinned, and come short of the glory of God." As Christians, we sin by commission and omission. John says in Revelation 12:10 that Satan is the accuser of the Christian, accusing them day and night. He tempts one to sin, belittles them when they yield to sin, and reminds them of their failure every chance he gets. Satan does this because he knows we are not perfect!

A Christ-centered home is a home where mom and dad and children, who have reached the age of accountability, know Christ as their Savior and seek to serve Him as their Lord. Dad, does your life demonstrate that the Spirit of God leads you? How long has it been since your family heard you pray or read the Bible? When was the last time you came home from church and shared with your family how the Lord blessed you through the sermon, the Sunday school lesson, or the music? When was the last time you shared with your family how the Lord had used you to win someone to Christ? When was the last time your family heard you say on Sunday evening or Wednesday evening, "Hurry up now, it is almost time for us to leave to go to church"? Dad, when was the last time you slipped down the hall at night, sat down on the side of your child's bed, and said, "Is there anything you would like for me to pray about?"

I asked these questions one Sunday morning in a revival service in south Alabama. During the invitation on Monday evening, a man stepped out from his pew and proceeded down the aisle with his daughter holding tightly to his hand. After the pastor shared the decisions that were made that night with the congregation, he said of this man's daughter, "This beautiful young lady comes tonight to share with you that she has accepted Christ as her Savior. Her dad had the joy of leading her to Christ last night."

The father of this young girl came to me after the services and said, "Thank you for what you shared with me yesterday morning. My daughter was one of many who came tonight to say she had accepted Christ into her heart. When you asked yesterday morning if I had ever asked my daughter if she had something she would like for me to pray with her about, I knew I had never done that. Her mother has been the one to put her to bed and pray with her at night. They always pray that little prayer, 'Now, I lay me down to sleep.' When my wife had placed our daughter in bed last night after the revival service, they shared their prayer time together. I slipped into my daughter's room, sat down on the side of her bed, and reminded her of what you said about praying with her concerning the needs of her life." Through his tears, he said, "Brother Don, my daughter began to cry. She said, 'Dad, I have been wanting to ask you how to be a Christian, but I didn't know how to ask you. I was afraid to ask you what I needed to do. Will you tell me how I can become a Christian?'" After a moment or two, he said, "Leading my daughter to know Christ as her Savior is one of the greatest experiences I have ever had in my life. Thank you, Brother Don, for sharing God's Word with us."

Are you a Christian mom? Does your life demonstrate that the Spirit of God controls you? Does your family ever hear you pray or read the Bible? Has your family ever seen you weep over the lost or unchurched? Have your children accepted Christ as their Savior? Do you ever talk with them about their spiritual relationship with Christ? When was the last time you asked your children if they had a friend they would like for you to pray with them about? Have you ever shared your experience of coming to know Christ with your children? Have you ever shared with your children how you and their dad know God's will for your lives and marriage?

"How old must a child be before they can become a Christian?" This is a question parents, who desire a Christ-centered home, ask me often. The Bible does not give a specific age one must reach before they become accountable for their sin. However, some believe the age of accountability is twelve, based on the age of Jesus when His parents took Him to the temple in Jerusalem, as recorded in Luke 2:42. "And when he was twelve years old, they went up to Jerusalem after the custom of the feast." Luke also shares with us in Luke 2:46 that when Joseph and Mary became separated from Jesus, they found Him in the temple, ". . . sitting in the midst of the doctors, both hearing them, and asking them questions." This passage of Scripture has led many to believe the age of accountability to be twelve. However, I believe one becomes accountable for their sin when the convicting Spirit of God makes them knowledgeable that they are a sinner. I have met many over the years, since entering evangelism, who have shared with me that they came to know Christ by age seven. Parents need to be mindful of the fact: if a child dies after they have reached the age of accountability, without accepting Christ as their Savior, that child will not go to heaven.

Parents are to teach their children the Word of God. In Proverbs 22:6, Solomon says, "Train up a child in the way he should go: and when he is old, he will not depart from it." This verse shares three truths parents are to observe in teaching God's Word to their children. First, Solomon reveals the procedure of teaching a child. He says, "Train up a child." For parents to train their child in biblical truths, they must share with them verbally and illustrate those truths through their daily lives. Children need consistency from their parents. A child always will learn more from what their parents are than from what their parents say. Parents also must involve their children in practical application of the truths they are trying to teach them.

The second truth Solomon shares is in the phrase "in the way he should go" (Prov. 22:6). The primary purpose for all teaching is to show the right way. In that the objective of a parent is to provide the best life possible for their children, teaching them about Christ and His Word is imperative. Jesus says in John 10:10, ". . . I am come that they might have life, and that they might have it more abundantly." Mom and Dad, are you teaching your children about Christ and His Word?

The third truth reveals the prize of teaching. Note the phrase, ". . . and when he is old, he will not depart from it" (Prov. 22:6). The prize of teaching is experiencing the benefits of the lessons learned. Listen to what Solomon says in Proverbs 3:13-26 about what one has when he has obtained the wisdom of God.

> Happy is the man that findeth wisdom, and the man that getteth understanding. For the merchandise of it is better than the merchandise of silver, and the gain thereof than fine gold. She is more precious than rubies: and all the things thou canst desire are not to be compared unto her. Length of days is in her right hand; and in her left hand riches and honour. Her ways are ways of pleasantness, and all her paths are peace. She is a tree of life to them that lay hold upon her: and happy is every one that retaineth her. The LORD by wisdom hath founded the earth; by understanding hath he established the heavens. By his knowledge the depths are broken up, and the clouds drop down the dew. My Son, let not them depart from thine eyes: keep sound wisdom and discretion: So shall they be life unto thy soul, and grace to thy neck. Then

shalt thou walk in thy ways safely, and thy foot shall not stumble. When thou liest down, thou shalt not be afraid: yea, thou shalt lie down, and thy sleep shall be sweet. Be not afraid of sudden fear, neither of the desolation of the wicked, when it cometh. For the LORD shall be thy confidence, and shall keep thy foot from being taken.

No wonder David can say in Psalm 37:25, "I have been young, and now am old; yet have I not seen the righteous forsaken, nor his seed begging bread." No wonder Solomon can say in Proverbs 3:5-6, "Trust in the LORD with all thine heart; and lean not unto thine own understanding. In all thy ways acknowledge him, and he shall direct thy paths." Mom and Dad, are your children being taught the Word of God by what you say and by the example of your life?

What would you say about your marriage?

If you and I could talk, and your mate could not hear our conversation, what would you say about your marriage? Would you say, "My wife and I have a good marriage. We know God's will and we are striving daily to accomplish it"? What would you say about your children? Would you say, "We are raising our children in accordance to the principles of God's Word, and we are leading them to know Christ and His will for their lives"? This is God's desire for every marriage; however, when you consider the spiritual depravity of America, you must conclude that many marriages are not accomplishing God's will.

Would you say, "Our marriage is dull"? Marriages have a tendency to become dull when the husband and wife become focused on material things and forget that life is short and what really counts in life are relationships. Recently, when the news media was interviewing families after a devastating tornado, a man said, "This tornado has taught me what is important in life. My wife and I have lost every material thing we ever had, but we have each other. That is all that counts." Life is short! David reminds us in Psalms 118:24, "This is the day which the LORD hath made; we will rejoice and be glad in it."

Many couples make their marriage dull by not providing quality time for one another. When was the last time you and your mate went out to a special place for dinner? When was the last time you and your mate took a few days of vacation, just the two of you? Do you ever go shopping with her? Do you ever go fishing, hunting, or golfing with him? Is there something both of you could enjoy doing together? Wishing for a better relationship will not change a dull marriage. If your marriage is dull, you must make some changes.

If you and I were talking about your marriage, and no one could hear our conversation, would you say, "I don't know if I love my mate or not"? Would you say, "I don't know if my mate loves me or not"? In a world where confusion and distortion are so prevalent, it is difficult to distinguish what is real and what is unreal. Hollywood has sold many a bill of goods concerning love. In 1 Corinthians 13, Paul shares a definition of real love. In the King James Version of the Bible, *love* is translated as "charity," but the Greek word is *agape* and refers to a God-like love. In describing his definition of love in 1 Corinthians 13:4-8, Paul says:

> Charity suffereth long, and is kind; charity envieth not; charity vaunteth not itself, is not puffed up, doth not behave itself unseemly, seeketh not her own, is not easily provoked, thinketh no evil; rejoiceth not in iniquity, but rejoiceth in the truth; beareth all things, believeth all things, hopeth all things, endureth all things. Charity never faileth . . .

In a perfect world, the love one has for his mate would always be pure. However, in a world stained by sin, one's love for their mate can become cold. Satan is capable of deceiving couples into believing they do not love their mate or never did. If this is something you are dealing with, examine what Paul says in Philippians 4:6-8.

> Be careful for nothing; but in every thing by prayer and supplication with thanksgiving let your requests be made known unto God. And the peace of God, which passeth all understanding, shall keep your hearts and minds through Christ Jesus. Finally, brethren, whatsoever things are true, whatsoever things are honest, whatsoever things are just, whatsoever things are pure, whatsoever things are lovely, whatsoever things are of good report;

if there be any virtue, and if there be any praise, think on these things.

In Ephesians 5:25, Paul challenges the husband to love his wife: "Husbands, love your wives, even as Christ also loved the church, and gave himself for it." In 1 Peter 3:7, Peter also challenges the husband: "Likewise, ye husbands, dwell with them according to knowledge, giving honour unto the wife, as unto the weaker vessel, and as being heirs together of the grace of life; that your prayers be not hindered." In Titus 2:4, speaking of the responsibility of older Christian women, Paul says, "That they may teach the young women to be sober, to love their husbands, to love their children." You cannot be the deacon or deacon's wife you should, if your love for your mate is in doubt.

Every marriage faces problems

Several years ago, in a premarital counseling session, I asked a young couple if they knew God's will for their marriage. As with the overwhelming majority of couples I have shared with in premarital counseling, this couple had no idea. When I asked, "If you and your husband live together for fifty years, how will you know your marriage has been successful?" The young woman said, "We can say we have had a successful marriage if we have been happy." I asked her, "Are you saying that your marriage will be successful if every day of your marriage will be a happy day?" She said, "Yes! I believe that would be true for every marriage."

I said, "In light of your definition for a successful marriage, let me ask you another question. What kind of world would we be living in if every day was a sunshiny day?" She said, "It would be a wonderful world, wouldn't it?" I said, "No! If every day was a sunshiny day, we would be living in a desert." I tried to share with that young couple that, as storms are a part of nature, so are problems a part of marriage. How we respond to our problems makes the difference in our marriage. Success in a marriage is not measured by what a couple has or by the moments of happiness they experience, but by their accomplishment of God's will together.

The problem many marriages face is the problem of not having dealt with the past. One evening a couple in their early twenties came into my office for their first premarital counseling session. I talked with them for a few moments, trying to calm their fears, and then I began to ask them some questions. I asked the young man, "Who was the authority figure in your home? Who was the disciplinarian? How were you disciplined? Who handled the money? If you wanted to go somewhere special, which parent would make that decision?" We discussed each of these questions. When I finished asking the young man these questions, I asked the same questions of the young woman, and I discussed each question with her.

When we had finished with these questions, I said, "You have some serious potential problems in your marriage." Angrily, the young woman responded. "What do you base that assumption on?"

I said, "Because you are coming from two completely different backgrounds. For the past twenty-two years, your fiancé was raised in a home where his father was the authority figure. His father was the disciplinarian, and he disciplined by spanking. His father was responsible for paying the bills and was the one who gave permission for special events. For the past twenty-two years, you were raised in a home where your mother was the authority figure. Your mother was the disciplinarian, and she disciplined by taking things away from you or putting you in quiet time. Your mother handled the money and was the one who gave permission for special events. Now, what are you going to do when your first child reaches the age to be disciplined and your husband spanks him/her? Who is going to be the authority figure in your home? Who is going to handle the money? Who is going to make the decision for the special events that will affect your children? The problem your marriage faces is how you are going to resolve the differences between how you were raised and how your husband was raised." She gave me a startled look and said, "We had not thought about these things." Most couples don't think of them.

I am sure there are other issues of the past we could discuss. However, that is not my intent. I want to encourage you to examine anything from your past that would prevent your marriage from being all God would have it be. It is impossible for a couple to accomplish God's will while dragging their past from day to day. As God reveals things to you that you need to change, you should do as Paul suggests in

Philippians 3:13-14, ". . . this one thing I do, forgetting those things which are behind, and reaching forth unto those things which are before, I press toward the mark for the prize of the high calling of God in Christ Jesus."

Another problem marriages face is the misunderstanding of the role of the husband and wife. Solomon says in Proverbs 18:22, "Whoso findeth a wife findeth a good thing, and obtaineth favour of the LORD." The problem arises when the husband and wife do not treat each other as God requires. How should a husband treat his wife? The husband is to love his wife (Eph. 5:25), honor his wife (1 Pet. 3:7), and live joyfully with his wife (Eccles. 9:9).

How is the wife to treat her husband? Paul reminds the wife in Titus 2:4 that she is to love her husband. A problem in many marriages is the biblical requirement for a wife to love her husband. In Ephesians 5:22, Paul says, "Wives submit yourselves unto your own husband, as unto the Lord." Again, in Colossians 3:18, Paul adds, "Wives, submit yourselves unto your own husbands, as it is fit in the Lord." For many women today, the idea of a wife submitting herself to her husband seems foolish.

The question often asked by those who think it foolish to submit to their husband is, "Why should I be the one who submits?" As a Christian, a wife is to be obedient to God's Word. She submits to her husband because God commands her to submit. God's plans always are anchored on a foundation. In God's plan for the home, the husband is to be the spiritual leader. God gives the husband the responsibility to lead his family to accomplish God's will for their lives. In 1 Corinthians 11:3, Paul says, "But I would have you know, that the head of every man is Christ; and the head of the woman is the man; and the head of Christ is God."

To clarify, the husband is the spiritual leader in the home. The Bible draws a parallel between Christ and His church and a husband and his wife. In Revelation 21:2, John identifies the church as the bride of Christ. He says, "And I John saw the holy city, new Jerusalem, coming down from God out of heaven, prepared as a bride adorned for her husband." In Revelation 21:9, John adds, "And there came unto me one of the seven angels which had the seven vials full of the seven last plagues, and talked with me, saying, Come hither, I will shew thee the bride, the Lamb's wife." Clearly, the Bible reveals the church to be the bride of Christ. The Bible also reveals that Christ is the head, or spiritual leader, of the church. Paul says in Colossians 1:18, speaking of Christ, "And he is the head of the body, the church: who is the beginning, the firstborn from the dead; that in all things he might have the preeminence." It is with this understanding that Paul shares in Ephesians 5:22-24:

> Wives, submit yourselves unto your own husbands, as unto the Lord. For the husband is the head of the wife, even as Christ is the head of the church: and he is the saviour of the body. Therefore as the church is subject unto Christ, so let the wives be to their own husbands in every thing.

In Ephesians 5:28-33, Paul sums up the parallel between Christ and His church to that of a husband and his wife by saying:

> So ought men to love their wives as their own bodies. He that loveth his wife loveth himself. For no man ever yet hated his own flesh; but nourisheth and cherisheth it, even as the Lord the church: For we are members of his body, of his flesh, and of his bones. For this cause shall a man leave his father and mother, and shall be joined unto his wife, and they two shall be one flesh. This is a great mystery: but I speak concerning Christ and the church. Nevertheless, let every one of you in particular so love his wife even as himself; and the wife see that she reverence her husband.

A wife's obedience to her husband enables her to be a greater witness for the cause of Christ. It is through obedience that one magnifies the Lord. Moses reminds us in Deuteronomy 27:10 that when one becomes a follower of God they are to ". . . obey the voice of the LORD thy God, and do his commandments and his statutes . . ." The Bible does not say that the wife is to be treated as a slave, nor as a mate of inferior value. In light of God's requirements for how a husband is to treat his wife, there can be no better, safer, or happier place for a wife than in the home of a husband who loves and serves the Lord.

Therefore, there is no problem within a marriage that cannot be solved, if both husband and wife are willing to address the problem honestly and be willing to allow the Holy Spirit to guide them toward a solution. Blaming the other mate will not solve problems. If a deacon and his wife are to do the work of the Lord, they must have a right relationship with Christ and a right relationship with their family. If they are not right in these two areas of their life, they are not right.

Permit me to ask you about your relationship with your family. Can you say your family relationship is pleasing to God? Does God's Spirit have control in your home? If the Spirit is quenched in your home, the absence of spiritual power will be evidenced in every aspect of your family's life. How do others view you with your family? Are you striving to help your family be all God would have them to be? Is there something spiritually missing in your family? Do you know what that something is? What are you willing to do to accomplish the will of God for your family? Are you willing to begin doing what God would have you do today?

Chapter 3

The Deacon in Relation to His Church

What is the role of the deacon in the church? Is the deacon to be, as some believe, the one who keeps the pastor "straightened out"? Are the deacons the collective voice of the church, speaking and acting on its behalf about its needs and direction? Just what is a deacon to do? Churches often elect church leaders and fail to provide them with spiritual training. Many of our churches have assumed that men, who are spiritually qualified to be elected as deacons, are knowledgeable of what is required of them to accomplish their task. This is a wrong assumption that often has proven injurious to the individual deacon and to the body of Christ.

When a man is elected a deacon and placed into service, he most often will begin to emulate what he sees other deacons doing, good or bad. The fault for not receiving the proper training for a deacon is twofold. First, it is the fault of the church for not demanding and providing the training for the deacon before he is ordained. Second, the deacon also must assume responsibility for not demanding that he be trained to serve as a deacon. No one can drive a car or fly a plane without instructions. Yet, being a deacon is far more complicated and demands a far greater skill.

Acts 8 gives an insight to the condition of the early days of the church. Luke says in Acts 8:1 ". . . And at that time there was a great persecution against the church which was at Jerusalem; and they were scattered abroad throughout the regions of Judaea and Samaria, except the apostles." Church history reveals that the members of that early church suffered persecution. They lost their jobs, their inheritances, and they were subject to physical abuse. However, despite the problems these early Christians faced, the church grew.

The persecution and financial problems the early church experienced, because of outside forces, made meeting the needs within the church extremely difficult. Those church members who were able to provide for the needs of their own family were encouraged to bring what they had to spare to the church, to provide for those who had nothing. However, a serious problem arose within the church concerning these provisions. God ordained the ministry of the deacon to solve this problem. Luke shares in Acts 6:1-4:

> And in those days, when the number of the disciples was multiplied, there arose

a murmuring of the Grecians against the Hebrews, because their widows were neglected in the daily ministration. Then the twelve called the multitude of the disciples unto them, and said, It is not reason that we should leave the word of God, and serve tables. Wherefore, brethren, look ye out among you seven men of honest report, full of the Holy Ghost and wisdom, whom we may appoint over this business. But we will give ourselves continually to prayer, and to the ministry of the word.

Both Grecians and Hebrews made up the membership of this early church. The Grecian members became upset; they believed the Hebrew widows were receiving a disproportionate amount of the daily offerings. Their murmuring caused a serious problem within the church. Something had to be done to address this problem. Seven men were chosen and were elected by the church to respond to this need.

It is of interest to note who these seven men were. Luke identifies them in Acts 6:5: ". . . and they chose Stephen, a man full of faith and of the Holy Ghost, and Philip, and Prochorus, and Nicanor, and Timon, and Parmenas, and Nicolas a proselyte of Antioch." All but one was a Jew. Luke specifically tells us Nicolas was a proselyte from Antioch. He was a Gentile, who had converted to Judaism and then became a Christian. The Bible does not tell us about Prochorus, Nicanor, Timon, or Parmenas.

However, the Bible does share with us about Stephen and Philip. Stephen is mentioned seven times in the New Testament, and Philip is mentioned more than thirty times. Stephen must have been a special individual to Luke, for he says of him in Acts 6:8, "And Stephen, full of faith and power, did great wonders and miracles among the people."

The task assigned to these first deacons required men well thought of by both the Grecians and the Hebrews. The church was looking for men of spiritual integrity and soundness. They were to be men that exemplified godly character in their private, as well as in their public, life. The church needed men who understood their role and were willing and able to do what was required of them. Both the Grecians and Hebrew members needed men they could trust to do what was right. Their very lives depended upon the actions of these seven men—so it is today. Churches and communities need their deacons to be men they can trust to share the Bread of Life . . . men that strive to be like Stephen, full of faith and spiritual power.

What are the qualifications of a deacon?

The first qualification of a deacon is that he has a right relationship with Christ. He must be saved and Spirit-filled. His assurance concerning his salvation must be settled, if he is to serve effectively. However, there are those who believe that if you are saved, then you will never doubt your salvation. I do not believe this. Paul tells us in 2 Corinthians 13:5 "Examine yourselves, whether ye be in the faith; prove your own selves. Know ye not your own selves, how that Jesus Christ is in you, except ye be reprobates?" If a Christian should never doubt his relationship with Christ, why would he need to examine his personal relationship with Him? John the Baptist was the forerunner of Christ. He saw Christ, had the experience of baptizing Him, and heard the audible voice of God identify Christ. This experience is recorded in Matthew 3:13-17.

> Then cometh Jesus from Galilee to Jordan unto John, to be baptized of him. But John forbad him, saying, I have need to be baptized of thee, and comest thou to me? And Jesus answering said unto him, Suffer it to be so now: for thus it becometh us to fulfil all righteousness. Then he suffered him. And Jesus, when he was baptized, went up straightway out of the water: and, lo, the heavens were opened unto him, and he saw the Spirit of God descending like a dove, and lighting upon him: And lo a voice from heaven, saying, This is my beloved Son, in whom I am well pleased.

In spite of all that John had seen, heard, and knew about Jesus, he had his doubts as to who He was. In Mark 6, John was imprisoned because of his preaching against the adulterous affair Herod was having with his brother Philip's wife Herodias (Mark 6:17-18). Just before John was beheaded, Luke records in Luke 7:19: "And John calling unto him two of his disciples sent them to Jesus, saying, Art thou he that should come? or look we for another?" Some assume that they are not spiritual if they say they have doubts about their salvation. The deacon, like all Christians, is subject to doubts. When doubts arise, a deacon must deal with those doubts if he is to be effective for Christ.

There are thirteen qualifications outlined for the office of the deacon found in Acts 6:3-8 and 1 Timothy 3:8-13. Let us note these qualifications.

1ˢᵗ — A deacon is to be a man of honest report (Acts 6:3).

A deacon is to have a good reputation among the members of his church, as well as those in his community who are not members of his church.

When I was in a revival some years ago, a man shared the following story with me. He said, "Brother Don, out here in the country, we all use the local grocery store/service station as our Wal-Mart. Last Saturday morning, I went by to purchase something. When I arrived, the parking lot was filled with cars and trucks. I parked around in the back, went in, and asked the owner if he had what I needed. He said, 'If I have that, it would be in the back on the bottom shelf.' As I was searching for what I came for, all those in the store left, leaving only myself and the owner remaining in the store. I heard someone come in. I recognized his voice when he spoke to the owner. He could not see me. He thought only he and the owner were in the store. In a loud voice, he said, 'Guess what my [curse word] church did for me this past Sunday.' The owner tried to tell him I was there, but he did not understand his hints. He told the owner again, 'Guess what my [curse word] church did for me last Sunday.' The owner replied, 'I don't know. What did they do for you?' The man said, 'My [curse word] church ordained me a deacon!' I stood up, and when he recognized me, his face turned white and out the door he went. Brother Don, the owner of the store is lost. Several of us in the community have been trying to win him to Christ. This vulgar-mouthed individual has caused this man so much harm that we may never reach him for Christ." I asked the man who told me this story if he had called the pastor of this deacon and shared with him what had taken place. He said, "Not yet, but I am going to tell him soon." This deacon's lifestyle does not indicate he has an "honest report" among those of his church or community.

2nd—A deacon is to be a man who is full of the Holy Spirit (Acts 6:3).

What does it mean to be "full of the Holy Spirit"? In simple terms, to be "full of the Holy Spirit" means that a Christian is allowing the Holy Spirit to control and empower his life. We get an understanding of the importance of being Spirit-filled when we consider the last words Jesus spoke to His disciples, just prior to His return to heaven. His disciples had been with Him for the past three years. They had heard Him preach and teach. They had observed the miracles He performed. He had just commissioned them to carry the gospel to the world. Were they ready to go? Not yet! Jesus told His disciples there was something else they needed before they were to go and share the gospel. What was so important that they could not go without it? In Luke 24:49, Jesus tells His disciples, "And, behold, I send the promise of my Father upon you: but tarry ye in the city of Jerusalem, until ye be endued with power from on high." They needed the power in their lives that only the Holy Spirit could provide.

The promise Jesus spoke of in this passage is the gift of the Holy Spirit. The word *endued* means "put on" (*Merriam-Webster's Collegiate Dictionary,* 10th ed.). The Spirit-filled life for the Christian comes by allowing the Spirit, by faith, to encompass or clothe his life with His presence. It is only when we are filled with the Spirit that our life can produce the "much fruit" God requires of us. Without the Spirit controlling our life, we have no spiritual power. Is your life controlled by the Spirit?

3rd—A deacon is to be a man full of wisdom (Acts 6:3).

Wisdom cannot be obtained by osmosis. Spiritual wisdom comes through prayer, Bible study, and experiences learned through the application of God's Word in our daily life. It is impossible to obtain spiritual wisdom without an understanding of who God is and developing a reverential fear of Him. To fear God seems strange for some. However, we must fear Him if we are to obtain the wisdom necessary to do His work. The author of Hebrews says, in Hebrews 12:28, "Wherefore we receiving a kingdom which cannot be moved, let us have grace, whereby we may serve God acceptably with reverence and godly fear."

To serve God, we need to know what He loves and hates. His ultimate love is for those who are lost. John 3:16 reminds us, "For God so loved the world, that he gave his only begotten Son, that whosoever believeth in him should not perish, but have everlasting life." Our love for God should cause us to love what He loves. We too are to love the lost and do all we can to win them to Christ.

Solomon, in Proverbs 6:16-19, reveals to us some of the things God hates.

> These six things doth the LORD hate: yea, seven are an abomination unto him: A proud look, a lying tongue, and hands that shed innocent blood, an heart that deviseth wicked imaginations, feet that be swift in running to mischief, a false witness that speaketh lies, and he that soweth discord among brethren.

God hates sin. God revealed His hate for sin by sending of His Son to the cross.

The effective deacon is one who strives daily to know and to do God's will. James 4:17 says, "Therefore to him that knoweth to do good, and doeth it not, to him it is sin." Wisdom is best evidenced through action. Does your life demonstrate that you are led by the wisdom of God?

4ᵗʰ — A deacon is to be a man full of faith (Acts 6:8).

Having accepted Christ by faith, the deacon is to walk in faith. What does the phrase "full of faith" mean for you? From the spiritual perspective, faith is more than a belief in something or someone. True faith involves the complete commitment of one's life. It involves the death of self. Paul describes his commitment of faith to Christ in Galatians 2:20 by saying, "I am crucified with Christ: nevertheless I live; yet not I, but Christ liveth in me: and the life which I now live in the flesh I live by the faith of the Son of God, who loved me, and gave himself for me."

In Romans 6:1-6, Paul reminds us that as Christians we are dead to self:

> What shall we say then? Shall we continue in sin, that grace may abound? God forbid. How shall we, that are dead to sin, live any longer therein? Know ye not, that so many of us as were baptized into Jesus Christ were baptized into his death? Therefore we are buried with him by baptism into death: that like as Christ was raised up from the dead by the glory of the Father, even so we also should walk in newness of life. For if we have been planted together in the likeness of his death, we shall be also in the likeness of his resurrection: Knowing this, that our old man is crucified with him, that the body of sin might be destroyed, that henceforth we should not serve sin.

Paul reminds us that the only way one can live by faith is to die to self and become dependent upon the indwelling Spirit of God to guide and direct our life. What would you say about your faith level? Can you say with Paul, "I can do all things through Christ which strengtheneth me" (Phil. 4:13)?

5ᵗʰ—A deacon is to be a man who is grave (1 Tim. 3:8).

The word *grave* refers to being honorable, honest, thoughtful, serious, and of a godly character. Thus, a deacon is to be a man whose character is above reproach. A pastor friend and I were playing golf one day. We came in behind a group of five men. It did not take but a moment or two to realize these men were not good at the game of golf. However, it was difficult for us to determine if their game was bad because they were bad golfers or because of the amount of beer they had consumed. To make matters worse, they were gambling. Every shot was examined carefully, in order that the bet made on that shot would be understood and fair to the other players.

As we waited, two other golfers caught up with us. We could hear them talking as they approached. One was using some rather foul language. When they arrived and saw what the players ahead of us were doing, they asked if they could play on through with us. I said, "Yes, if you do not mind playing with two Baptist preachers." The one who had been using the foul language said, "We will be glad to play with you Baptist preachers; I am a deacon in my church." I said, "I thought I heard you say something about that when you were driving up." His friend turned to him and said, "I have told you. You need to watch your language." This was not a man "grave" or of godly character.

It is imperative that deacons, along with all Christians, live a life that is ever-pleasing to God. Christians are the only example of Christ that many people will ever know.

6th — A deacon is to be a man who is not
"double-tongued" (1 Tim. 3:8).

A person who is "double-tongued" is deceitful and scheming. Often he will say one thing and do another. In James 1:8 we are reminded, "A double minded man is unstable in all his ways." Several years ago, a pastor friend shared with me that the deacons in the church he was serving asked him to resign. He said, "The meeting became ugly. The deacons were telling me how bad my preaching was and that I was a very poor pastor. I was in the home of the deacon that was most vocal against me on the previous Friday evening. He had gone out of his way to tell me how much he loved me. He said I was not only the best preacher he ever heard, but no pastor visited his church members more than I did. Now, he was leading the charge against me. When I asked him if he was the same man who told me the previous Friday how much he loved me and how great a preacher and pastor I was, he never answered."

David asks in Psalms 15:1-3,

Lord, who shall abide in thy tabernacle? who shall dwell in thy holy hill? He that walketh uprightly, and worketh righteousness, and speaketh the truth in his heart. He that back-biteth not with his tongue, nor doeth evil to his neighbour, nor taketh up a reproach against his neighbour.

Sometimes the phrase "speaking out of both sides of their mouth" carries with it the same idea of being "doubled-tongued." I have met a few deacons who spoke well of their pastor in his presence, but spoke harshly of him in his absence. These same deacons were for both sides of issues that arose in the church. Their position on these issues depended on whom they were with and what the people they were with thought about these issues. Such action creates division and is not of God.

7ᵗʰ—A deacon is to be a man not given to much wine (1 Tim. 3:8).

In our society, there is a great deal of emphasis placed on the phrase, "not much wine." Several years ago, there was an hour-and-a-half debate at the Southern Baptist Convention on the subject of whether or not drinking was a sin. Solomon shares in Proverbs 20:1, "Wine is a mocker, strong drink is raging: and whosoever is deceived thereby is not wise." In Proverbs 23:29-35 Solomon adds,

Who hath woe? who hath sorrow? who hath contentions? who hath babbling? who hath wounds without cause? who hath redness of eyes? They that tarry long at the wine; they that go to seek mixed wine. Look not thou at the wine when it is red, when it giveth his color in the cup, when it moveth itself aright. At the last it biteth like a serpent, and stingeth like an adder. Thine eyes shall behold strange women, and thine heart shall utter perverse things. Yea, thou shalt be as he that lieth down in the midst of the sea, or as he that lieth upon the top of a mast. They have stricken me, shalt thou say, and I was not sick; they have beaten me, and I felt it not: when shall I awake? I will seek it yet again.

The arguments by those who favor drinking say these verses are from the Old Testament and have no relevance for today. They point out that 1 Timothy 4:4 reveals that everything God created is good and is to be received. Those who favor drinking are quick to remind others that the first miracle Jesus performed was turning water into wine at the wedding of Cana in Galilee, as recorded in John 2. However, they fail to mention that turning water into wine was not the purpose for the miracle. Jesus performed this miracle to illustrate that His coming into the world was to fill empty lives with meaning and purpose. Those in favor of drinking also are quick to remind others that wine is good for medicinal purposes, quoting 1 Timothy 5:23: ". . . use a little wine for thy stomach's sake and thine often infirmities."

One night after a revival service, a man approached me. He was upset because of comments I made about Christians drinking. He said, "So, you think drinking is a sin?" "Yes, I do," I answered. He responded, "The Bible does not say that drinking is a sin!" "Is that what you believe?" I asked. He proceeded to give me chapter and verse of why he believed drinking was not a sin. When he had finished, I said, "Sir, can I ask you a question?" "Go ahead," he said. I said, "Last night after the revival service was over, many from the church went out to a local restaurant to eat. You and your wife also went. Do you and your wife eat at that restaurant often?" "Yes, we do! It is close to home and the food is good," he answered. I said, "I would imagine they serve alcoholic beverages at that restaurant. Do they?" With a big smile on his face, he said, "Yes, they do. And I usually enjoy a good cold beer when I go there to eat." I said, "I noticed you didn't drink one last night. May I ask you why you did not?" Again, with a big smile on his face, he said, "Because I have too much respect for my pastor to drink in his presence." I said, "You mean to tell me you have more respect for your pastor than you do for the Lord?" Angrily, he said, "What do you mean by that?" I said, "You just told me when you and your wife go to that restaurant to eat, you usually enjoy a cold beer. Sir, the Lord is there when your pastor is not. The Lord is omnipresent. He is everywhere all the time. You said you had too much respect to drink in front of your pastor. Doesn't it bother you to drink in the Lord's presence?"

As he turned to walk away, I said, "Sir, can I ask you one more question?" He did not answer. He just shook his head in the affirmative. "You said drinking is not a sin. Would you say telling a lie is a sin?" He thought for a moment and said, "Yes. It is wrong to tell a lie. Lying is a sin." I said, "Did you know the constitution and by-laws of this church say, 'As members of this church, we will abstain from the sale and use of alcoholic beverages'?" After a moment, he said, "Brother Don, you have given me a great deal to think about. Thank you!" The next night after the service, his wife left him talking with some of his friends and came over to where I was. She said, "Thank you for sharing with my husband last night. He is a good man. He knows drinking is wrong. He just wants somebody to tell him it is alright for him to drink."

Should a deacon drink? Paul says in 1 Corinthians 8:13, "Wherefore, if meat make my brother to offend, I will eat no flesh while the world standeth, lest I make my brother to offend." Deacons should set an example in all they do. Do you drink? With whom do you choose to drink? Are you the example you should be as a deacon?

*8ᵗʰ—A deacon is to be a man who is not greedy
(1 Tim. 3:8).*

In a world of "want," few are satisfied with what they have. However, there is nothing wrong with wanting or having things. The problem comes when we are controlled by wanting and having things. Listen to the wisdom of Solomon in Proverbs 30:7-9, as he reveals how to address this issue.

Two things have I required of thee; deny me
them not before I die: Remove far from me
vanity and lies: give me neither poverty nor
riches; feed me with food convenient for me:
Lest I be full, and deny thee, and say, Who is
the LORD? or lest I be poor, and steal, and
take the name of my God in vain.

The owner of the business where I was employed
before entering the ministry was a man considered
to be a greedy individual. Many of his employees
believed his goal in life was to earn "just one more
dollar." As I was witnessing to a fellow employee
one day, he asked, "Isn't the owner of this business
a deacon in the largest Baptist church in town?" I
said, "Yes, he is." He said, "Do you think he is a
Christian?" I said, "I hope he is." His next statement
startled me. He said, "You have been asking me to
give my life to Christ. You have talked with me about
getting my family in church, so we could all go to
heaven. I just want to say if the owner of this business is going to heaven, I had rather go to hell." We
forget sometimes that we are the only Christ some
know and the only Bible some read.

*9th—A deacon is a man who loves God's Word and
practices its truths (1 Tim. 3:9).*
   This qualification for the deacon requires "holding
the mystery of the faith in a pure conscience" (1 Tim.
3:9). To a lost person, the truths of God's Word are
foolishness. The lost person may say they believe
God's Word, but genuine faith always is associated

107

with genuine action. The actions of the lost person indicate they do not believe their sins have separated them from God. They do not believe the biblical teaching that reveals that God became flesh, was born of a virgin, lived a sinless life, was crucified for our sins, rose again, and will return to earth for those who have accepted Him as their Savior.

Herein is the "mystery of faith." We that are saved have been sanctified by faith (Acts 26:18), justified by faith (Rom. 3:28), and have access to God by faith (Rom. 5:2). As Christians we live by faith (Rom. 1:17) and stand by faith (1 Cor. 16:13). The mystery of faith is not something to be kept, but something to be shared. As such, what a deacon believes about God's Word is imperative to his spiritual walk with Christ. If the deacon is weak in his understanding of God's Word, or reluctant to stand on or share God's truths, he is not worthy of being a deacon. His love for the truth of God's Word cannot be contrived. That love must be genuine and must demonstrate itself through his daily life.

In a world of political correctness, we need men of God who know God's Word and have the courage to stand on it. Pastors, especially young pastors, need deacons who will encourage them to share God's truths to a lost and dying world. What does God's Word mean to you? Meditate with David in Psalm 119:103-106.

How sweet are thy words unto my taste! yea, sweeter than honey to my mouth! Through thy precepts I get understanding: therefore

I hate every false way. Thy word is a lamp unto my feet, and a light unto my path. I have sworn, and I will perform it, that I will keep thy righteous judgments.

10th—A deacon is a man who has been proven (1 Tim. 3:10).

When it came time to elect new deacons in the first church I pastored, the church chose two men in their early twenties. Both of these young men had been Christians for more than a year. However, in a deacons' meeting prior to their election by the church, one older deacon voiced his opposition. He said, "I think it is wrong for this church to ordain these two boys." When another deacon asked him why he felt as he did, the older deacon said, "They are just too young." Then another deacon spoke. He said, "I have never known men who are more mature and faithful to Christ than these two men are. We should be honored to serve with them." The older deacon replied, "It doesn't matter how faithful they are now. The question is how faithful will they be in years to come?" When someone shared with the older deacon that both of these young men were more faithful than he was, he became angry.

Indeed, there needs to be sufficient time for a man to prove himself, but how long is long enough? The Bible does not give a specific age that a man must be before he can be ordained a deacon, nor does the Bible reveal how long one must be a Christian before he is eligible to be a deacon. The Bible does say in 1 Timothy 3:6 that he is not to be a new convert: "Not a novice, lest being lifted up with pride he fall into the condemnation of the devil."

11ᵗʰ—A deacon is to be a man who is blameless (1 Tim. 3:10).

To be "blameless" is to be a man who walks in the commandments and ordinances of the Lord. Such a man is not guilty of sinful living. He lives a life characterized by holiness. No one can bring an accusation of wrong against him that will stand. He knows who he is and what he believes, and he is faithful to his convictions. A godly deacon will follow the example of Peter when others falsely call his character into question. Note what Peter says in 1 Peter 2:20-23:

> For what glory is it, if, when ye be buffeted for your faults, ye shall take it patiently? but if, when ye do well, and suffer for it, ye take it patiently, this is acceptable with God. For even hereunto were ye called: because Christ also suffered for us, leaving us an example, that ye should follow his steps: Who did no sin, neither was guile found in his mouth: Who, when he was reviled, reviled not again; when he suffered, he threatened not; but committed himself to him that judgeth righteously.

12ᵗʰ—A deacon is a man who is the husband of one wife (1 Tim. 3:12).

Is Paul telling us a deacon can have only one wife at a time? Is Paul reminding us of the prohibition against polygamy? Is he saying that a divorced man cannot be a deacon? Is Paul saying an ordained deacon who experiences a divorce should resign? Is Paul saying a man must be married to be a deacon? What does the "husband of one wife" mean? Without doubt, this is the most controversial of all the qualifications for the deacon.

I believe the qualification of being the husband of one wife means that if a man is married or has been married, he must not have two wives in God's sight. God's design for marriage is found in Genesis 2:24. Moses tells us, "Therefore shall a man leave his father and his mother, and shall cleave unto his wife: and they shall be one flesh." In God's original design for marriage, there was to be one man and one woman, for a lifetime. However, the Bible reveals that God's plan for marriage has not always been followed.

Does God forbid divorce? Is divorce always considered a sin? We are told in Genesis 21 that Abraham was commanded by the Lord to divorce Hagar (Gen. 21:12). Some would argue that Hagar was Abraham's handmaid, but Genesis 16:3 calls her his wife. In Ezra 9 and 10, Ezra tells the Israelites that God commanded them to divorce their foreign wives.

Consider what God says about divorce in Jeremiah 3:6-8:

> The LORD said also unto me in the days of Josiah the king, Hast thou seen that which backsliding Israel hath done? she is gone up

upon every high mountain and under every green tree, and there hath played the harlot. And I said after she had done all these things, Turn thou unto me. But she returned not. And her treacherous sister Judah saw it. And I saw, when for all the causes whereby backsliding Israel committed adultery I had put her away, and given her a bill of divorce; yet her treacherous sister Judah feared not, but went and played the harlot also.

In Jeremiah 3:11-13, God promises to take Israel back if she will, "Only acknowledge thine iniquity, that thou hast transgressed against the LORD thy God, and hast scattered thy ways to the strangers under every green tree, and ye have not obeyed my voice, saith the LORD" (Jer. 3:13).

These verses reveal that divorce is not always a sin. In Genesis 21, when God instructs Abraham to divorce Hagar, there is no stipulation given to Abraham not to take another wife. In fact, Genesis 25:1 says after the death of Sarah, Abraham married Keturah. Some would argue that this was alright because it was after Sarah's death. Do not forget Hagar and the fact that Abraham had other concubines as well (Gen. 25:6). Is God pleased with divorce? No! Malachi 2:16 tells us, "For the LORD, the God of Israel, saith that he hateth putting away . . ."

Deuteronomy 22:13-19 reveals that before a man could divorce his wife he had to have a just cause. In Deuteronomy 24:1-4, we see that a just cause could be that the husband had found some "uncleanness in her." The different interpretations of the phrase "some uncleanness in her" has caused divisions down through the ages. In the day of Christ, the conservative school of Shammai understood the phrase to mean adultery. Yet, Leviticus 20:10 reminds us adultery was punishable by death. On the other hand, the liberal school of Hillel taught that the phrase implied that a wife could be divorced by her husband if she burned his food or if he saw a woman who pleased him more.

There are several important truths, found in Deuteronomy 24:1-4, that are relevant to our discussion concerning divorce and remarriage. First, let us note this Scripture passage.

> When a man hath taken a wife, and married her, and it come to pass that she find no favour in his eyes, because he hath found some uncleanness in her: then let him write her a bill of divorcement, and give it in her hand, and send her out of his house. And when she is departed out of his house, she may go and be another man's wife. And if the latter husband hate her, and write her a bill of divorcement, and giveth it in her hand, and sendeth her out of his house; or if the latter husband die, which took her to be his wife; her former husband, which sent her away, may not take her again to be his wife, after that she is defiled; for that is abomination before the LORD: and thou shalt not cause

the land to sin, which the LORD thy God giveth thee for an inheritance.

This passage of Scripture clearly teaches that the husband and wife were divorced. She was the guilty party because her husband found "some uncleanness in her." However, the husband gave her a "bill of divorcement," and their marriage was dissolved. It is also clear that the wife could marry again, by virtue of the statement, ". . . she may go and be another man's wife." The bill of divorcement served as a legal notification that their marriage was dissolved. When she married another man and he too divorced her, he also gave her a bill of divorcement to show proof of his legal divorce. She could not return to her first husband because she was defiled.

Now, move forward into the New Testament and examine what Jesus had to say about this passage of Scripture. Jesus made His comments concerning this passage in the region of Judea. It was not accidental that the Pharisees brought up the subject of divorce with Jesus in Judea at this time. Herod Antipas, the governor of that region, had just divorced his wife to marry Herodias. Herodias was both his sister-in-law, the wife of his brother Philip, and his niece, the daughter of his brother Arstobulus. The Pharisees were hoping Jesus would express His conservative view on divorce, Herod would hear about it, and he would behead Jesus as he had beheaded John the Baptist (Matt. 14:10). Now, note Matthew 19:3-6:

The Pharisees also came unto him, tempting
him, and saying unto him, Is it lawful for a
man to put away his wife for every cause?
And he answered and said unto them, Have
ye not read, that he which made them at the
beginning made them male and female, and
said, For this cause shall a man leave father
and mother, and shall cleave to his wife: and
they twain shall be one flesh? Wherefore they
are no more twain, but one flesh. What therefore God hath joined together, let not man put
asunder.

The plan of the Pharisees failed because Christ
inverted their question. They asked, "Is it lawful for
a man to put away his wife for every cause?" (Matt.
19:3). Instead of answering their question, Jesus
asked them a question that pointed them back to the
basic biblical definition of marriage (Matt. 19-4-5).

Matthew shows the Pharisees' persistence in
attempting to entrap Jesus by quoting some Scripture
of their own (Matt. 19:7). They reminded Jesus that
Moses, the lawgiver, had sanctioned divorce, quoting
from Deuteronomy 24:1-4. Jesus acknowledged that
divorce occurred during the days of Moses, because
of their forefathers' hard hearts. Jesus corrected their
theology further by reminding them that Moses did
not "command" divorce; rather, he "suffered" divorce
(Matt. 19:8). It is important to note that Jesus, in His
explanation on divorce, took the Pharisees back to
the Genesis account of marriage and reminded them

divorce was never God's intent. He said, ". . . but from the beginning it was not so" (Matt. 19:8).

Paul says in Romans 7:1-3 that when a mate dies, the other mate is free to remarry. Some would argue there are two other exception clauses found in the New Testament, granting the innocent mate the right to remarry after a divorce. The first of these is "fornication," as noted in Matthew 5:32. Jesus says, ". . . whosoever shall put away his wife, saving for the cause of fornication, causeth her to commit adultery." Thus, when a mate commits an adulterous act, the innocent mate has the option to exercise the exception clause and seek a divorce. Those who hold this view believe the innocent mate has every right to remarry, because the marriage was dissolved on spiritual grounds.

The second exception clause is "desertion." This clause is illustrated in 1 Corinthians 7:15. In this passage, Paul is referring to a Jewish family, in which the wife embraced Christ but her husband did not. The husband was so adamant against Christ that he not only refused Christ, but also was willing to divorce his wife for her acceptance of Him. Paul says, "But if the unbelieving depart, let him depart. A brother or sister is not under bondage in such cases: but God hath called us to peace" (1 Cor. 7:15).

Let me reiterate my interpretation of what Paul means when he says, "the husbands of one wife" (1 Tim. 3:12). I believe the requirement for the deacon, concerning having only one wife, is that if a man is married or has been married, he must not have two wives in God's sight. In other words, if his divorce or the divorce of his wife does not fall under the exception clauses outlined in Scripture, he is not to be a deacon.

13ᵗʰ—A deacon is to rule his children and house well (1 Tim. 3:12).

If a marriage is to be successful, the husband must understand his relationship as spiritual leader for his wife. He is to love her, honor her, and treat her according to the instruction of God's Word (1 Pet. 3:7). A leader is one who knows where he is, where he is going, and how to get there. The spiritual leader is to lead his family to fulfill God's will for their lives. The decisions necessary to accomplish this task will not always be easy for him to make, nor for his family to receive. For a husband to know how to lead his family, he must have a right relationship with Christ and be led by His Spirit.

The word *rule* means "to exert control, direction, or influence on" (*Merriam-Webster's Collegiate Dictionary,* 10ᵗʰ ed.). A deacon is required to rule his children well. How is he to do this? He begins by living a life that exemplifies what he desires his children to become. He exalts Christ and trains his children in the truths of God's Word. He gives his children time. He becomes involved in their personal life. Their schoolwork becomes important to him. He encourages them in their relationship with Christ through Bible study and prayer. He demonstrates his love to his children by word and action.

For the deacon to "rule his children well," he must have the respect of his children. Respect cannot be demanded or forced; it must be earned. The role of a father is an extension of the role of the heavenly Father. The objective of every father should be to accomplish the challenge given by Solomon in Proverbs 22:6: "Train up a child in the way he should go: and when he is old, he will not depart from it."

Continually proven

The office of the deacon requires more than simply meeting the qualifications to be a deacon. The actions of a deacon are always under scrutiny. Once a man has proven himself worthy of being chosen and elected a deacon, his commitment to Christ and his responsibilities as a deacon are to be proven continually. In 1 Timothy 3:13, Paul says of the ordained deacon, "For they that have used the office of the deacon well purchase to themselves a good degree, and great boldness in the faith which is in Christ Jesus." God will reward the deacons who are faithful in their responsibilities. They will receive a "good degree." In the eyes of others, they will be viewed as men of God because they serve Him faithfully. Their spiritual prowess will afford them greater opportunities to serve God. The church is a blessed church that has men serving as deacons who use the office well.

Should a woman be a deacon?

Each of the qualifications for a deacon, given by Luke in Acts 6 and by Paul in 1 Timothy 3, are directed to men. There is a clear distinction made between the deacon and the deacon's wife in 1 Timothy 3:11. This verse illustrates that the qualifications for a deacon are for a man: "Even so must their wives be grave, not slanderers, sober, faithful in all things." By the phrase, "Even so," Paul marks a distinction between the deacon and the deacon's wife.

Some argue that Phoebe is proof that women should be ordained as "deaconesses." From a biblical perspective, anything said about Phoebe, other than what is noted in Romans 16:1, must be argued from silence. Some speculate there were women in the first church who were known as "deaconesses." Many believe these women ministered exclusively to other women, but did not function in the same capacity as male deacons. Others speculate that a "deaconess" was the wife of a deacon. I believe the Bible is clear on this issue. Both Luke, in Acts 6, and Paul, in 1 Timothy 3, identify the gender of the deacon to be that of a male. Of all the popular versions of the Bible, only the Revised Standard Version calls Phoebe a deaconess.

Training for the deacon is imperative

As I stated in the beginning of this chapter, churches often elect deacons and fail to provide them with training. The word *train* means "to form by instruction, discipline, or drill" (*Merriam-Webster's Collegiate Dictionary,* 10th ed.). Training involves having a clear vision, becoming organized, or becoming committed to a task. First, before a deacon is trained, he must be given a clear vision of his objective. To understand the purpose for the deacon ministry in your church, there must be an understanding for the purpose of your church.

Once, when I came to a church to serve as pastor, I asked, "What is the purpose for our church?" You would have thought I had asked the most foolish question ever asked. Several responded, "Everyone knows the purpose for every church is to win the lost in their community to Christ." I asked, "Is that all we are to do? What should we do about meeting physical, financial, and emotional needs of those in our community? What is our purpose concerning missions within our association, our state, and around the world? What are we to do with those we win to Christ? Are we to disciple them? Are we to assist those who answer God's call to full-time Christian service?"

Winning the lost to Christ is paramount to the overall purpose of the church. However, there is more to being a church than winning the lost to Christ. I asked this church to formulate a Long Range Planning Committee. The purpose for this committee was to identify needs and formulate a plan for meeting those needs. After several months of hard work and much prayer, the committee reported their findings to the church. The church evaluated the recommendations made by the committee and asked the committee to condense their findings to a "Statement of Purpose." The statement of purpose was adopted and gave the members of the church a clear vision that they could accomplish.

When a church has a clear vision concerning God's will, it is ready to organize the members to accomplish that purpose. It is ready to make decisions concerning which ministries and programs are to be started. The order by which each ministry and program is started is important. Who will serve on the various ministries and programs? The church must make decisions as to the funding of each of the ministries and programs. There must be a clear understanding for the objective of each ministry and program, as well as how they will be charted.

The third ingredient of training involves acquiring the knowledge for the planned work and sharing that knowledge with those to do the work. Before a deacon can be effective, he must know what the church would have him do. No matter his dedication, his concern, his desire to serve, or his spiritual abilities, he must know what is required of him. He needs a job description and he needs training for the job he is to do. In that deacons are the primary "care-takers" of the church, they need training in visiting hospitals, shut-ins, and nursing home patients. Deacons need training in their ministry as church greeters, helping the pastor administer the Lord's Supper, baptisms, and receiving the church offerings. They need training as "soul winners." Deacons also need training in assisting the pastor to counsel those who come forward during the invitations, at the conclusion of the worship services.

There is no "board" of deacons

The relation of the deacon to his church involves an understanding of the deacon's position in the body of Christ. In many Baptist churches, the phrase "board of deacons" refers to more than an official body. This phrase implies a governing board. In churches where the deacons view themselves as authority figures, they often believe their role is to keep the pastor "straightened out." These deacons see themselves as the collective voice of the church, speaking on matters of doctrine and direction, oftentimes without the consent or knowledge of the church as a whole. There is no scriptural foundation for this action. Luke states in Acts 6 that the church chose and elected the first deacons. It was the church who instructed those first deacons as to what they were to do and how they were to accomplish their responsibilities. It should be the same for deacons today. Deacons are accountable to the church, not the church to the deacons.

What takes place in most deacons' meetings might cause one to doubt those deacons who say they are accountable to the church. In the deacons' meeting of most Baptist churches, the time is spent considering reports from the various committees of the church. If you ask why, one deacon will say, "It has always been done this way." Another deacon may say, "This is done in order that we stay informed as to what is going on in our church."

In my first deacons' meeting in a church I served as pastor, I sat and observed how the men conducted their meeting. I wanted to know how they viewed themselves. Were they servants of the church or a "governing board?" It did not take me long to find out. As the secretary for the deacons read his report from the previous meeting, I noticed that most of the deacons served as a member on a committee of the church. One by one, they presented to the deacons the report their committee would be sharing with the church in the next conference meeting.

When I stopped the secretary of the deacons and asked him what he was doing, he seemed startled. He said, "I am reading the minutes from the previous deacons' meeting." I said, "Do I understand that every committee in this church presents their report to the deacons before they are presented to the church?" One older deacon responded, "Yes! We have always done it this way. Is there a problem with that?" I said, "Before I answer your question, let me ask you why this is done." Another deacon responded, "In that we are the deacons, this is done to keep us informed as to what is going on in this church." I said, "If that is the case, why did you vote on these reports, giving them an up or down vote? Who authorized the deacons to tell the properties and grounds committee they could not change the locks on certain doors? Who authorized the deacons to tell the flower committee they could spend a certain amount of money each month for flowers?" One deacon said, "You are trying to take away all our authority." I said, "When did you ever have the authority to tell this church what it can and cannot do? This church elected these committees, and from now on, the reports from these committees will be shared with the church on conference night." Another deacon asked, "Then, how are we to know what is going on in the church?" I said, "By being in conference with the rest of us."

When the church assigns a responsibility to a committee, that committee is responsible to the church to accomplish their assignment. The responsibility of the deacons is not to take the oversight of each committee, telling them what and how to do their job. Each committee should have the opportunity to do their job on their own. There are more important matters to be discussed in deacons' meetings than hearing and voting on committee reports. The primary responsibility of the deacon is to help the pastor move the church in the spiritual direction God would have the church go. The deacons' meeting should be a time when the pastor shares with the deacons his objectives for advancing the cause of Christ. It should be a time devoted for discussion as to how the deacons can enhance the atmosphere of worship services. There should be time in the deacons meetings that is devoted to planning for the deacons to encourage every member to become involved in the work of the church. Deacons' meetings should be a time of joy. It should be a time when spiritual men meet to hear from their pastor concerning God's will for the advancement of His kingdom through their church.

I believe the reason some deacons have assumed more authority than they should have is not altogether their fault. In some cases, their church has permitted them to do as they have because the membership is content for someone else to be responsible for the work that is to be done. Another reason is noted: when pastors leave a church, someone must assume the leadership role. Often this responsibility falls on the shoulders of the deacons. However, when the new pastor is called by the church and he begins his ministry, he fails the deacons if he does not have the conviction and courage to take his position as undershepherd of the church. When the pastor is young and inexperienced, some deacons are reluctant to relinquish the role of under-shepherd to him, for fear he is not mature enough to do his job. Therefore, it is imperative that a church call the right pastor, and the deacons, by faith, perform their ministry of assisting him as he leads the church.

Create an infectious commitment for reaching people

The deacon's relation to his church is evidenced by his willingness to help the pastor establish a fellowship that communicates sincere love and acceptance for all who live within the church community. There can be no second-class prospects. All are people of worth! It is impossible for a church to minister to a community that it does not know. Demographics will tell you how many live in your community, their ages, their gender, their income, their educational level, their marital status, whether they are renting or buying their home, and their annual income, but it will not tell you their spiritual needs. The spiritual needs of those in your community are discovered by personal contact, and this will not happen unless people care. Deacons are to set the example for caring and responding to these needs. In order to win some to Christ, you first must win their confidence. You must convince them you really care about them.

The last church I pastored, before entering evangelism, was Liberty Baptist Church, located in College Park, Georgia. Because of the encroachment of the Atlanta airport, families who had lived in the area for more than twenty-five years were moving out. As they moved out and new families moved in, our community became racially diverse. Soon we added more than seventy-five African Americans and more than one hundred and fifty Cambodians to our average Sunday school and worship attendance each week. Our deacons in this ministry assisted Mrs. Barbara Jarrell, our director of Cambodian Ministry. They set the example in visiting and ministering to the needs of our community.

I have been in hundreds of churches since I entered evangelism. I have met deacons who started:

- A ministry that provided transportation to their church for those who lived in local nursing homes
- A ministry that provided communion services for patients in nursing homes and the local hospice facility
- A ministry that provided classes for those in their community who needed to know how to
  - Cook and sew
  - Play an instrument
  - Work on computers
  - Speak English
  - (All these ministries were for sharing Christ!)

The best way to win someone to Christ is show them you care about them.

How can the requirements for the deacon in your church be determined?

As I conduct deacon retreats across America, I often am asked, "How can our church determine a job description for our deacons?" A job description for the deacon becomes easier to define when the will of God for the church is made clear. It is only when a church has discerned how God would have the church minister to its members, community, and its purpose around the world that a job description can be formulated for the deacons. The church has the responsibility of identifying God's plan for its existence and subdividing that plan into a workable format, which can be implemented by its members. Thus, a job description should communicate clearly and concisely what responsibility each job entails and the qualifications and attributes each person must have to perform that job.

Once your church formulates God's plan for ministry, deacons should be assigned a specific role to aid in the success of each task. This does not mean they are to lead each committee or program. As deacons, their role may be to assist or encourage a certain group or committee, providing them with support. Ask the average pastor, "What is your greatest need?" Most often he will say, "Getting my people motivated to do what God requires of them." A deacon can assist the pastor at this point by being assigned to a specific task within the church to garner the support of those needed to accomplish that task.

Deacons do not always have to be in a leadership role. Being an example sometimes is of more value than being a leader. For some deacons to live the example, changes are necessary. Some deacons may need a new *determination*. What about your determination? Will you today determine to do more to be the example God would have you be? Desire is the key! You must want to do God' will if God's will is to be accomplished.

Some deacons need a new *direction*. Where are you and your family on Sunday and Wednesday evening? Are you in church? Where are you when the offering plate is passed? Do you tithe? Where are you when it comes time to share your faith? When was the last time you led anyone to Christ?

Some deacons need a new *dependence*. David says in Psalm 118:8, "It is better to trust in the LORD than to put confidence in man." Don't assume you can't do what God would have you do or that you can't encourage others to do better. Do as Solomon says in Proverbs 3:5: "Trust in the LORD with all thine heart; and lean not to thine own understanding." Remember you were chosen to serve as a deacon because other church members observed your spiritual strength.

Some deacons need a new *dedication*. How devoted are you to God and the accomplishing of His will? The times in which you and I live are tough and getting tougher! Kids are killing kids. The bigger a liar you are and the more perverted you are, the more the world loves you, whether you be politician or preacher. I am convinced that the condition of our world is due to the fact that many church members are not as dedicated to God as they should be. It is time men of God stood up and shouted with their voice and with their actions, "Here I am, O God, use me!" Our world needs men who are responsible to God, to their families, to their friends and neighbors. James 1:22 says, "But be ye doers of the word, and not hearers only, deceiving your own selves."

Before I close this chapter, permit me to ask you several questions.

1. How do you rate yourself as a deacon?
2. Are you helping or hurting the growth of your church?
3. Are you a source of encouragement or discouragement?
4. What, if anything, do you need to change in your life, within the context of your relationship with your church?

Permit me to ask the deacon's wife some questions.

1. How do you rate yourself as a deacon's wife?
2. Are you helping or hurting the growth of your church?
3. Are you a source of encouragement or discouragement?
4. What, if anything, do you need to change in your life, within the context of your relationship with your church?

Chapter 4

The Deacon in Relation to His Pastor

The relation of the deacon to his pastor begins with an understanding of the position of the pastor in the body of Christ. The pastor is the under-shepherd of the church. The word *pastor* is translated from the original Greek word *poimen*. The familiar Anglo-Saxon word *shepherd* is also a translation of this word. The root meaning of this word is "one who tends the sheep" (*Merriam-Webster's,* 10th ed.) Other names for the pastor include "elder" or "presbyter," from the Greek word *presbuteros* and *bishop,* or "overseer," from the Greek word *episcopos*.

Qualifications for the pastor

Paul shares with us the qualifications for the pastor in 1 Timothy 3:1-7 and Titus 1:5-9. In 1 Timothy 3:1-7, Paul shares:

This is a true saying, if a man desire the office of a bishop, he desireth a good work. A bishop then must be blameless, the husband of one wife, vigilant, sober, of good behaviour, given to hospitality, apt to teach; not given to wine, no striker, not greedy of filthy lucre; but patient, not a brawler, not covetous; one that ruleth well his own house, having his children in subjection with all gravity; (For if a man know not how to rule his own house, how shall he take care of the church of God?) Not a novice, lest being lifted up with pride he fall into the condemnation of the devil. Moreover he must have a good report of them which are without; lest he fall into reproach and the snare of the devil.

The apostle Paul repeats these qualifications of a bishop/elder/pastor (the same Greek word *episkopos* is used) in his letter to Titus.

For this cause left I thee in Crete, that thou shouldest set in order the things that are wanting, and ordain elders in every city, as I had appointed thee: If any be blameless, the husband of one wife, having faithful children not accused of riot or unruly. For a bishop must be blameless, as the steward of God; not selfwilled, not soon angry, not given to wine, no striker, not given to filthy lucre; but a lover of hospitality, a lover of good men, sober, just, holy, temperate; holding fast the

faithful word as he hath been taught, that he
may be able by sound doctrine both to exhort
and to convince the gainsayers.

—Titus 1:5-9

Let's take a moment and examine these
qualifications.

1ˢᵗ — The basic qualifications for the pastor:

1. Must be a Christian (John 3:7)
It should never be assumed that a prospective
pastor is a Christian. Ask him! Ask him to tell you
about his conversion. Ask him to tell you how his life
has changed since he became a Christian. Ask him
to tell you what he believes becoming a Christian
involves. Ask him about his burden for the salvation
of others. Jesus says in Matthew 7:21, "Not every
one that saith unto me, Lord, Lord, shall enter into
the kingdom of heaven; but he that doeth the will of
my Father which is in heaven." No genuine Christian
I know would be offended by being asked about his
relationship with Christ.

2. Must be a male (1 Tim. 3:1; Titus 1:6)
"If a man desire the office of a bishop, he desireth
a good work" (1 Tim. 3:1). The idea that the ministry
of the pastor be restricted to a man is, without doubt, an
issue debated by many in the church today. However,
this is not an issue of chauvinism or discrimination.
It is an issue of biblical interpretation. I believe the

Bible clearly teaches that men are to be the spiritual leaders within their home and the church.

Though women, just as much as men, are called to minister to others, to demonstrate the fruit of the Spirit (Gal. 5:22-23), and to proclaim the gospel to the lost (Matt. 28:18-20; Acts 1:8; 1 Pet. 3:15), there are no biblical references to a woman serving as pastor. Neither is there Scripture that suggest that women pastors should be considered the norm. Paul, in speaking of ministry within the church, says in (1 Tim. 2:11-12), "Let the woman learn in silence with all subjection. But I suffer not a woman to teach, nor to usurp authority over the man, but to be in silence."

3.   Not a novice (1 Tim. 3:6)

What is a novice? The word novice, in this text, means one who is a new convert. It may also mean one who is to inexperienced to be a pastor. Nearly every profession has guidelines as to when an individual is permitted to make personal decisions concerning his occupation. An electrician has three or four years of training and an additional three to five years of apprenticeship before becoming a master electrician. A plumber has at least five years of apprenticeship before getting a master plumber certificate. This is true for carpenters and other tradesmen. A physician requires eight years of education beyond high school and three to eight years of internship and residency before he/she can have the full privileges of a doctor.

What are the requirements for a pastor? In the Southern Baptist Convention, there are no educational or experience requirements. Some would argue that if God calls someone to pastor, God will equip him. In Acts 9, we note the conversion and call of Paul to preach. Examine carefully Acts 9:20-22, "And straightway he preached Christ in the synagogues, that he is the Son of God. But all that heard him were amazed, and said; is not this he that destroyed them which called on this name in Jerusalem, and came hither for that intent, that he might bring them bound unto the chief priests? But Saul increased the more in strength, and confounded the Jews which dwelt at Damascus, proving that this is very Christ."

Do these verses contradict Paul's statement that a pastor should not be a novice? No! Preaching is one thing, pastoring a church involves more than just being able to preach. Paul's statement that a pastor should not be a novice is a warning against becoming a pastor and being controlled by pride rather than by God's Spirit. Satan will do all he can to make a young preacher fail. Success in the pastorate has caused many preachers to be so filled with pride that they have assumed themselves to be of more value than they are. It is a wise congregation that seeks a pastor who has both experience and spiritual maturity to be their pastor.

4. Must desire the job (1 Tim. 3:1)

The Lord, undoubtedly, does call men; He places within their heart, by the work of His Spirit, a desire so strong for ministry they cannot be satisfied in any other calling. Consider God's call upon the life of

Jeremiah. In Jeremiah 1:5 we read, "Before I formed thee in the belly, I knew thee; and before thou camest forth out of the womb I sanctified thee, and I ordained thee a prophet unto the nations." Jeremiah's assurance of his calling is evidenced in Jeremiah 20. When Jeremiah was disappointed with the sinfulness of his nation and angry with God for not dealing with their sins, as Jeremiah saw them, he cried out to God and said, "O LORD, thou has deceived me, and I was deceived: thou art stronger than I, and hast prevailed: I am in derision daily, every one mocketh me. For since I spake, I cried out, I cried violence and spoil; because the word of the LORD was made a reproach unto me, and a derision, daily. Then I said, I will not make mention of him, nor speak any more in his name. But his word was in mine heart as a burning fire shut up in my bones, and I was weary with forbearing, and I could not stay" (Jer. 20:7-9). As Jeremiah considers the plight of his people and their lack of change, he cries out to to God, "I quit. I will not preach anymore." Yet, almost in the same breath, he says, "But His Word was in my heart like a fire in my bones, and I could not stop."

At the age of fourteen, lying on my grandmother's front porch in an old iron swing, the Lord called me to preach. From that moment on, I have had a burning desire to proclaim God's Word. I live to preach! I see spiritual needs and formulate sermons within my mind to meet those needs. I envision the lost, without Christ, going to hell, and my heart cries out with a message of change and hope. There is an old saying, "Some preachers are mama called and daddy sent." However, the preacher/pastor who will stay the course and preach the truth must know he has been called by God. He must desire the job.

5. Is faithful to the Word of God (Titus 1:9)

What does it mean for a pastor to be "faithful to the word of God?" It means that he is to live out the truth he preaches. When I was a boy, there was a pastor in our community who preached against "sins" that he and his family seemed to enjoy. It was said of this pastor, "He preaches one thing and lives another."

Faithfulness to God's Word requires study, discipline, and consistency. Paul, in 2 Timothy 4:2-4, says, "Preach the word; be instant in season, out of season; reprove, rebuke, exhort with all long suffering and doctrine. For the time will come when they will not endure sound doctrine; but after their own lusts shall they heap to themselves teachers, having itching ears; and they shall turn away their ears from the truth, and shall be turned unto fables."

We have come to the day when many in the church have itching ears and desire a pastor that will tell them what they want to hear, rather than what God's Word says. Blessed is the church that has a pastor who preaches and lives the truth of God's Word.

6. Apt to teach (1 Tim. 3:2)

There are no biblical requirements concerning the level of education for a pastor. However, he is to: "Study to shew thyself approved unto God, a workman that needeth not to be ashamed, rightly dividing the word of truth" (2 Tim. 2:15).

The ability of the pastor to teach God's Word is important to the growth of the church. To teach wisely, a pastor must study deeply, pray long, and know the needs of his flock. Studying is an arduous task! It requires desire, time, and effort. A pastor must not only know God's Word, but he also must be able to explain it to all who hear him, both the educated and uneducated, the young and the old.

A pastor should not only be able to teach God's Word, he also should be able to test his teaching. Teaching that does not change lives is not teaching. One way a pastor can test his teaching is to examine the changed lives of his members. If he is teaching his people they are to make disciples, he should ask himself, "How many more members does our church have this year than we had last year?" If he is teaching on tithing, he should ask, "How many more of our members tithe this year than tithed last year?" The answer to these and similar questions will inform the pastor as to the effectiveness of his teaching. Granted, teaching must be accepted and implemented by church members, but it is the responsibility of the pastor to teach.

7. Able to exhort and convince the lost
   (Titus 1:9)

It is a wise pastor who learns the truth: ". . . Not by might, nor by power, but by my spirit, saith the LORD of hosts" (Zech 4:6). In and of himself, the pastor can do nothing; he is dependent upon the Lord. However, knowing this truth does not alleviate a pastor from doing his best to preach convincingly and strive daily to win the lost to Christ.

The pastor cannot make people choose truth or accept Christ as their Savior. However, he does have the responsibility to present the gospel in an informative manner. His love and desire for the sinner will be evidenced by what he says and how he says it. Yet, there is more to being a pastor/teacher than sharing three sermons per week. A pastor's concern for the spiritual needs of his people is demonstrated through his ministry to them, visiting them in the hospital, at home, or in the nursing home. He conducts their marriages, is present at the birth of their children, and counsels with them when problems arise in their home. He weeps with them when their loved ones die and comforts them as he conducts the funeral. It is through his daily ministry to his people that a pastor illustrates his true desire for their spiritual needs.

2nd — The family qualifications for the pastor:

1. The husband of one wife (1 Tim. 3:2; Titus 1:6)

What does this statement mean? Are we to believe that a pastor must be married? Was Paul married? If marriage is a requirement for a pastor, why didn't Paul clarify his marital relationship? Paul never tells us about his wife. Some argue that Paul was married and refer to Paul's statement in 1 Corinthians 9:5: "Have we not power to lead about a sister, a wife, as well as other apostles, and as the brethren of the Lord, and Cephas?"

Others argue Paul was never married and refer to 1 Corinthians 7:1-7.

> Now concerning the things whereof ye wrote unto me: It is good for a man not to touch a woman. Nevertheless, to avoid fornication, let every man have his own wife, and let every woman have her own husband. Let the husband render unto the wife due benevolence: and likewise also the wife unto the husband. The wife hath not power of her own body, but the husband: and likewise also the husband hath not power of his own body, but the wife. Defraud ye not one the other, except it be with consent for a time, that ye may give yourselves to fasting and prayer; and come together again, that Satan tempt you not for your incontinency. But I speak this by permission, and not of commandment. For I would that all men were even as I myself. But every man hath his proper gift of God, one after this manner, and another after that.

In these verses Paul implies he had the gift of celibacy; thus, he was never married.

Does the statement "husband of one wife" refer to divorce? Some believe it does, and they take a strong stand on this issue. When God instituted marriages in the Garden of Eden, it was His plan that a marriage be unending (Gen. 2:24). In Malachi 2:16), speaking about divorce, Malachi says, "For the LORD, the God of Israel, saith that he hateth putting away . . ." In Matthew 19, when the Pharisees brought up the fact that divorces occurred during the days of Moses, Jesus responds by saying, ". . . Moses because of the hardness of your hearts suffered you to put away your wives: but from the beginning it was not so" (Matt. 19:8). Without doubt, the Bible clearly teaches that God hates divorce.

With this in mind, let me throw this caveat into the mix. In chapter two, I asked, "Are all 'marriages,' marriages?" Paul tells us, "Be ye not unequally yoked together with unbelievers: for what fellowship hath righteousness with unrighteousness? and what communion hath light with darkness?" (2 Cor. 6:14). From Scripture, we must conclude that marriage is a divine institution, and to be sanctioned by God, a marriage must meet God's requirements. What is to be the result of a marriage that does not meet God's requirements? Is there no biblical reason for divorce? Note Matthew 19:9, ". . . Whosoever shall put away his wife, except it be for fornication, and shall marry another, committeth adultery: and whoso marrieth her which is put away doth commit adultery." Jesus says if a mate commits fornication, there are grounds for divorce. He does not say the innocent party is not to remarry.

Some argue that the pastor is to be blameless. His life is to be above reproach. I agree. Sometimes there are circumstances over which one has no control. I have known two or three pastors whose marriages were dissolved, despite all their best efforts. One pastor's wife left him for another woman. Another pastor's wife lived in an adulterous lifestyle for years before she left him. This pastor found his wife in their bed with more than one man. He loved her and treated her with mercy and forgiveness. He endured her scandalous lifestyle for years. One day she filed for divorce and moved out of the house. Several years later, he remarried, and a number of pastors in his Association argued he was living in adultery. I don't think so! If the exception clause Jesus spoke about in Matthew 19 is good for a layperson, why does it not apply to the pastor?

The marital status of a prospective pastor is of great importance. The pulpit committee has an obligation to examine the marital status of their prospective pastor; after all, he is to lead his flock by example. If his marital status does not measure up to the biblical standard, he should be rejected.

2. Rules his house well (1 Tim. 3:4)

A C.E.O. of a large company shared with me, "If I had my choice, I would never interview a candidate for a position in my company. I would interview their children. A child's actions and manners will tell you volumes about the character of their parent." He was right! I also heard a teacher say, "Children hear more of what you are than what you say." She too was right. A pastor demonstrates his ability to manage and lead the church by how he conducts himself with his wife and children, and by how he conducts his home financially. Observe his relationship with his wife and children. How do his wife and children respond to him? Is he loving and caring, or are his actions coarse and harsh? Do his wife and children fear him or respect him? How do he and his wife live financially? Is his family living within their means?

Peter reminds us how a man is to treat his wife. "Likewise, ye husbands, dwell with them according to knowledge, giving honour unto the wife, as unto the weaker vessel, and as being heirs together of the grace of life; that your prayers be not hindered" (1 Pet. 3:7). Paul shares how a godly wife should respond to her husband. He said the wife is "To be discreet, chaste, keepers at home, good, obedient to their own husbands, that the word of God be not blasphemed" (Titus 2:5). These two verses describe a home where love and respect abounds, where God's will is desired and where both husband and wife strive to accomplish His will. This is the type of pastor a church should seek.

How do the pastor and his wife treat their children? Are his children respectful? How do they interact with others their own age? What of their attire? Are they neat and clean? Are these trivial questions that have no meaning? It should be remembered that the pastor is the spiritual leader of the church, and as he leads his family, he will lead the church.

3.   Has faithful children (1 Tim. 3:4; Titus 1:6)

Solomon is right when he says, "Train up a child in the way he should go: and when he is old, he will not depart from it" (Prov. 22:16). What a joy it is to see pastor's children love the things of God. In a recent revival, a minister of youth shared with me, "Our pastor's son is sixteen years old. He is one of the most faithful Christians I have ever known." This was not only a compliment bestowed upon this young man, but on his parents as well. The actions of a child will reflect the character of their parents.

No matter how well a man preaches or what his educational qualifications are, of far greater value is the spiritual condition of his family. He must lead his family by example. Solomon says, "If a man beget an hundred children, and live many years, so that the days of his years be many, and his soul be not filled with good, and also that he have no burial; I say, that an untimely birth is better than he" (Eccles. 6:3).

3rd—Lifestyle and pastoral qualifications:

1. Blameless (1 Tim. 3:2; Titus 1:7)

What is meant by the word blameless? Paul is saying that a pastor is to be a man who exemplifies a Christian character. It is sad to say, but we are living in a day when you can believe anything you want and live anyway you please and still be considered a good Christian by many. This idea may be prevalent, but it is not biblical. Jesus says, "My sheep hear my voice, and I know them, and they follow me" (John 10:27). He also says, ". . . If ye continue in my word, then are ye my disciples indeed; and ye shall know the truth, and the truth shall make you free" (John 8:31-32).

Blameless does not mean perfect. Paul reminds us, ". . . There is none righteous . . ." (Rom. 3:10). The word *blameless* does, however, mean that a pastor should live a life that is above reproach. There should be nothing in his life that will bring shame upon the name of Christ.

2. Vigilant (1 Tim 2:3)

The old adage is true that says, "Anything worth having is worth working for." Only a few people will ever realize the work and time involved in being a pastor. It is not uncommon for a pastor to spend forty hours per week on sermon preparation. In addition to preparing sermons, he is busy visiting, counseling, traveling, praying, and studying. Trying to balance time between his family's needs and his responsibilities at the church has caused many pastors to leave the ministry. Being a pastor is not an easy task!

When I am in a revival and the pastor tells me we are going over to someone's house for lunch, my first thought is, "I hope she loves to cook." I have discovered that when you eat with someone who loves to cook, you are blessed. The same is true with a pastor who loves what he does. What a joy to be around pastors who love their people and find it a blessing to minister to them. A church is blessed to have a pastor who loves them and who does not see his responsibilities as a chore to be avoided but a joy to be experienced.

3. Sober (1 Tim 3:2; Titus 1:8)

To be sober means to be sincere, or have a serious attitude concerning life. Paul does not imply that a pastor is not to have a sense of humor. If this were true, there would be no Baptist pastors, for how could anyone pastor a Baptist church and not have a sense of humor? Most Baptist preachers could write a book on the funny things they have seen and heard within the churches they have pastored.

It must be understood that there is a difference between the pastor who has a sense of humor and one who is a clown. The clown always must be the center of attention. He will say and do anything to get a laugh. When a clown is in the pulpit, there is no substance to his message. When he visits the sick, there is not much compassion for the hurting. When he visits the bereaved, most often it is with indifference. Blessed is the church that has a pastor who views life from the perspective of the Savior.

4. Good behavior (1 Tim 3:2)

A pastor is required to have and exercise good manners. He is to treat others with Christian respect and kindness. How one treats others is often a reflection of how he views himself. If a pastor treats others with contempt, he most often does so because he views himself as superior. A pastor must be confident but not cocky. Solomon reminds us: "A man that hath friends must show himself friendly: and there is a friend that sticketh closer than a brother" (Prov. 18:24).

5. Given to hospitality (1 Tim. 3:2; Titus 1:8)

The pastor is to be given to hospitality. What does this qualification involve? It means that a pastor has an obligation to lead his church to meet the needs of his congregation and community, whether those needs be social, physical, or spiritual needs. In order to do this, the pastor must possess the skills necessary to recognize these needs and the ability to organize and train his church members to meet these needs.

It takes a pastor with a shepherd's heart to know the needs of his church and community. No pastor can know his people if he does not mingle with them. He must know where they are spiritually if he is to help them grow spiritually. The sad truth is that most churches organize around what they *are* doing, rather than what they *should be* doing, and wonder why they are not going anywhere. It must be understood that church growth is not limited to what can be done within the church. If a church is to grow to its full potential, the pastor must lead his people to reach beyond the walls of the church. This is best done by ministering to the needs of the church and community from a biblical perspective.

6. Not given to wine (1 Tim. 3:3; Titus 1:7)

There are two views concerning this qualification. Some believe Paul says the pastor is to abstain from wine, and others believe Paul is saying a pastor should not be addicted to wine. I believe Paul is saying the responsibilities of the pastor are so grave that he cannot afford to allow anything to cloud his mind. The pastor must be clear in his thinking and ever ready to perform his responsibilities. I believe this is a command for the pastor not to consume alcohol.

Drinking wine in Paul's day was a common practice. However, most did not drink wine for its alcohol content. A student of history will note there were several reasons why the drinking of wine was such a common practice in this region of the world. There were many vineyards, and grapes were produced in abundance. In that there was no refrigeration system, the only way to preserve the juice from the grapes was to allow it to ferment. Sewage systems often were inadequate, and the drinking water in most cities was impure. The wine was mixed with water and boiled, thus purifying the water, removing the alcoholic effect and providing water with a better taste. Drinking to become drunk was a distasteful practice and was avoided by most Jews. Solomon says in Proverbs 20:1, "Wine is a mocker, strong drink is raging: and whosoever is deceived thereby is not wise."

7.   No striker (1 Tim. 3:3; Titus 1:7)

Being a leader is one of the most difficult responsibilities of a pastor. Lister to what the Lord asked Ananias to tell Paul at his conversion: "But the Lord said unto him, Go thy way: for he is a chosen vessel unto me, to bear my name before the Gentiles, and kings, and the children of Israel: For I will shew him how great things he must suffer for my name's sake" (Acts 9:15-16). Walk along the pages of the Bible with Moses, and you can clearly see the difficulty of leadership. It is obvious that both Paul and Moses had their moments of frustration and doubt. Like Jeremiah (Jer. 19:7-9), most pastors have had their days when they would have thrown in the towel gladly.

To be a pastor, one must have the conviction and courage to withstand the insults and criticisms of those being led, even when they do not understand or will not accept leadership. When a pastor preaches truth that some find offensive, he must be patient if they lash out with harsh and cruel words in frustration. There is no place in the pastorate for a bully. A pastor is unwise who chooses to use force to lead his people. A wise pastor knows it is easier to lead people who love and respect you, but love and respect are earned not demanded.

It also should be pointed out that a leader is not to be weak and vacillating in order to appease his people. Jeremiah says his nation fell, "For the sins of her prophets, and the iniquities of her priests, that have shed the blood of the just in the midst of her" (Lam. 4:13). A pastor must proclaim the truth and lead his people under the tutelage of the Spirit's guidance, with holy boldness and Christlike love.

8. Not greedy (1 Tim. 3:3)

One's appetite for things covers many different areas of life. For some it is materialism. They want money, houses, land, cars, things that they can feel and touch, things they can enjoy for the moment, or things they can display to others as a show of wealth. Others desire prestige, the applause and the acclaim of others. There is nothing wrong with the desire to achieve. Problems arise when achievement becomes an obsession. Even within the pastorate, there are men whose ambition in life exceeds God's will. Their desire for a bigger church, speaking engagements at the National Conventions, and the acceptance of certain preachers and Convention leaders becomes an obsession, and they will do anything to achieve their goal.

Paul says a pastor is to be content with what he has! In other words, don't be obsessed by what you want and don't have, but do your best with what you have and where you are. Paul said, "But godliness with contentment is great gain" (1 Tim. 6:6). A pastor should not spend his days complaining about his plight. Someone told me years ago, "Don't complain, don't condemn, and don't criticize, because most people don't care anyway."

9.   Patient (1 Tim. 3:3)

Some of these qualifications appear to be repetitive or overlapping. Yet, each one is noted for their importance and clarification. Paul speaks of the value of patience. He says, ". . . we glory in tribulations also: knowing that tribulation worketh patience; and patience, experience; and experience, hope: And hope maketh not ashamed: because the love of God is shed abroad in our hearts by the Holy Ghost which is given unto us" (Rom. 5:3-5). In Philippians 4:11-13, Paul says, ". . . for I have learned, in whatsoever state I am, therewith to be content. I know both how to be abased, and I know how to abound: every where and in all things I am instructed both to be full and to be hungry, both to abound and to suffer need. I can do all things through Christ which strengtheneth me."

A pastor will soon discover that every member of his congregation is uniquely different. He must patiently care for those who are reluctant to spiritual change, or slow to learn what he teaches. He must not carry a grudge or be slow to forgive. He will soon learn that every day is new, yet many days seem the same. The pastor is to, "Preach the word; be instant in season, out of season; reprove, rebuke, exhort with all long suffering and doctrine. For the time will come when they will not endure sound doctrine; but after their own lusts shall they heap to themselves teachers, having itching ears; and they shall turn away their ears from the truth, and shall be turned unto fables. But watch thou in all things, endure afflictions, do the work of an evangelist, make full proof of thy ministry" (2 Tim. 4:2-5).

10. Not a brawler (1 Tim. 3:3)

What is a brawler? A brawler is one who enjoys an argument. He is contentious and hard to get along with. A brawler is easy to anger and often unwilling to forgive and forget his offenders. Paul views a brawler as one who is in a state of carnality. "For ye are yet carnal: for whereas there is among you envying, and strife, and divisions, are ye not carnal, and walk as men?" (1 Cor. 3:3).

In 1 Timothy 6:3-6, Paul shares with us how a pastor is to teach without being contentious: "If any man teach otherwise, and consent not to wholesome words, even the words of our Lord Jesus Christ, and to the doctrine which is according to godliness; he is proud, knowing nothing, but doting about questions and strifes of words, whereof cometh envy, strife, railings, evil surmisings. Perverse disputing of men or corrupt minds, and destitute of the truth, supposing that gain is godliness: from such withdraw thyself. But godliness with contentment is great gain." Advice for the brawler is summed up in Philippians 2:3: "Let nothing be done through strife or vainglory; but in lowliness of mind let each esteem other better than themselves."

11. Not covetous (1 Tim. 3:3)

A covetous person is one who has a strong desire to possess something that belongs to someone else. This qualification is given to challenge the pastor to keep his focus on the things of God. As Jesus is sharing the parable of the rich fool, He says, ". . . Take heed, and beware of covetousness: for a man's life consisteth not in the abundance of the things which he possesseth" (Luke 12:15). Covetousness is a grave sin, and in Colossians 3:5, Paul calls covetousness idolatry.

In Paul's day, followers of Christ were most often very poor, and their pastors were bi-vocational. Money was scarce and needs were many. It was a time when Proverbs 3:5-10 took on a special meaning. "Trust in the LORD with all thine heart; and lean not unto thine own understanding. In all thy ways acknowledge him, and he shall direct thy paths. Be not wise in thine own eyes: fear the LORD, and depart from evil. It shall be health to thy navel, and marrow to thy bones. Honour the LORD with thy substance, and with the firstfruits of all thine increase: So shall thy barns be filled with plenty, and thy presses shall burst out with new wine."

12. Not a lover of money

Paul warns, "For the love of money is the root of all evil . . ." (1 Tim. 6:10). Paul does not say that money is the root of all evil, but the obsession for money is the evil associated with it. In that money is used as a bartering agent, there is nothing wrong with money or wanting or having it. Paul warns the pastor not to become obsessed with obtaining money. Once again, Paul's challenge to the pastor is for him to keep his focus on the Lord. Paul is telling him not to lose sight of what is most valuable, for there are more important things in life than money.

It is a sad state when a pastor becomes more concerned about the money he makes than the truth he preaches. A pastor should never be overly concerned if the truth of his message offends those in his church who hold the purse strings. Judas, the betrayer of Jesus, is a biblical example of one being more interested in money than he was in standing for the truth of Christ. "Then one of the twelve, called Judas Iscariot, went unto the chief priests, and said unto them, What will ye give me, and I will deliver him unto you? And they convenanted with him for thirty pieces of silver. And from that time he sought opportunity to betray him" (Matt. 26:14-16). A pastor should never be fearful to preach against sin for fear of losing his job.

13. Just (Titus 1:8)

The word *just* carries with it the idea of being honest. Have you ever known a pastor who was so inconstant he could change his mind on any subject, depending on who he was with at the moment? Paul's warning, in this qualification, is a reminder for the pastor to be consistent in his teaching and Christian living, no matter his circumstance. If a pastor disagrees with someone, he is to be honest. This can be done in a loving spirit.

David describes an honest man:

Lord, who shall abide in thy tabernacle? who shall dwell in thy holy hill? He that walketh uprightly, and worketh righteousness, and speaketh the truth in his heart. He that backbiteth not with his tongue, nor doeth evil to his neighbour, nor taketh up a reproach against his neighbour. In whose eyes a vile person is contemned: but he honoureth them that fear the LORD. He that sweareth to his own hurt, and changeth not. He that putteth not out his money to usury, nor taketh reward against the innocent. He that doeth these things shall never be moved.

—Psalms 15:1-5

14. Holy (Titus 1:8)

This qualification is a challenge to the pastor to become consecrated to God and separated from the world. Looking back over the past twenty to thirty years, it is amazing how the message of the pulpit has changed on many subjects. Drinking, homosexuality, cohabitation . . . all have become a part of the church and are seldom denounced from many pulpits, for fear of reprisals. A pastor is to preach the whole truth without fear or favor. He must remember that he is an ambassador of God. The pastor has no message, only God's. His lifestyle should exemplify Christlikeness in all that he says and does.

The pastor must separate himself from the world. John, in 1 John 2:16, says, "For all that is in the world, the lust of the flesh, and the lust of the eyes, and the pride of life, is not of the Father, but is of the world." Paul adds, in 2 Corinthians 6:17, "Wherefore come out from among them, and be ye separate, saith the LORD, and touch not the unclean thing; and I will receive you." It would appear that some pastors today are more interested in appeasing the world than in pleasing God. Blessed is the church that has a holy pastor.

These qualifications for the pastor, like those for the deacon, are not to imply the church is to find "perfect" individuals to fill these positions. While salvation occurs in an instant, Christians are works in progress. Paul, in Philippians 3:10-14, helps us understand that the goal for the pastor is to strive continually to be more of what Christ would have him be. He says:

> That I may know him, and the power of his resurrection, and the fellowship of his sufferings, being made conformable unto his death; if by any means I might attain unto the resurrection of the dead. Not as though I had already attained, either were already perfect: but I follow after, if that I may appre-hend that for which also I am apprehended of Christ Jesus. Brethren, I count not myself to have apprehended: but this one thing I do, forgetting those things which are behind, and reaching forth unto those things which are before, I press toward the mark for the prize of the high calling of God in Christ Jesus.

What are the responsibilities of the pastor to the church?

The responsibilities of the pastor to the church are threefold. First, pastors are to be the under-shepherd of the local church. As under-shepherd, the pastor is the spiritual leader of the church. Paul, in Acts 20:28, addresses this fact by sharing the following charge to pastors. He says, "Take heed therefore unto yourselves, and to all the flock, over the which the Holy Ghost hath made you overseers, to feed the church of God, which he hath purchased with his own blood." As the spiritual leader, the pastor is the overseer of the church. An *overseer* is one charged with the duty of seeing that things to be done by others are done well. He is a guardian of souls, one who watches over the welfare of others. In 1 Peter 5:2, Peter also addresses the pastor as the under-shepherd of the church by saying to them, "Feed the flock of God which is among you, taking the oversight thereof, not by constraint, but willingly; not for filthy lucre, but of a ready mind." Peter teaches that the pastor is not to lead his flock by force, nor for personal gain, but in a manner that honors and glorifies God.

Second, the pastor is to feed his sheep by preaching and teaching. Luke tells us, in Acts 28:31, that when Paul was imprisoned in Rome, he was involved in "Preaching the kingdom of God, and teaching those things which concern the Lord Jesus Christ, with all confidence, no man forbidding him." In 1Timothy 5:17, Paul addresses the responsibility of the pastor by saying, "Let the elders that rule well be counted worthy of double honour, especially they who labour in the word and doctrine." Paul reveals that the pastor who is faithful in his preaching and teaching will receive a double honor.

There is a difference between preaching and teaching. Preaching has a narrower meaning than teaching. *Preaching* is the sharing of the gospel with the intent of converting the unconverted. *Teaching* is the explanation and clarification of the gospel to those who have accepted Christ. Like most preachers, Paul seems to have had his greatest success as a teacher. He spent a year and six months at Corinth, "teaching the word of God among them" (Acts 18:11). After Paul taught two years at Ephesus, ". . . all they which dwelt in Asia heard the word of the Lord Jesus, both Jews and Greeks" (Acts 19:10). That experience may have been on his mind when Paul wrote to Timothy, saying, ". . . the things that thou hast heard of me among many witnesses, the same commit thou to faithful men, who shall be able to teach other also" (2 Tim. 2:2).

Third, the pastor is to be an example to his flock. First Peter 5:3 reminds the pastor, "Neither as being lords over God's heritage, but being examples to the flock." As the under-shepherd, the pastor is to exemplify the Great Shepherd. Isaiah prophesied the title of "Great Shepherd" of Christ. In Isaiah 40:11, we read, "He shall feed his flock like a shepherd: he shall gather the lambs with his arm, and carry them in his bosom, and shall gently lead those that are with young." In John 10:11, Jesus fulfilled this prophesy when He said, "I am the good shepherd: the good shepherd giveth his life for the sheep." The under-shepherd, like the Great Shepherd, is to love his sheep compassionately and sacrificially.

The pastor is not to become a dictator, ruling with a heavy hand. He is to understand that God has given him his position as pastor. The sheep that he is to lead and feed are not his, but rather they belong to God, purchased by the blood of His Son (Acts 20:28). It is from this perspective that the pastor is to love, feed, and lead the sheep he serves. He is to protect and provide for their spiritual needs. He is to warn them of impending danger and correct them when they are rebellious.

It must be understood there is a difference between a shepherd and a hireling. Jesus draws a sharp contrast between the two in John 10:11-15:

> I am the good shepherd: the good shepherd giveth his life for the sheep. But he that is an hireling, and not the shepherd, whose own the sheep are not, seeth the wolf coming, and leaveth the sheep. The hireling fleeth, because he is an hireling, and careth not for the sheep. I am the good shepherd, and know my sheep, and am known of mine. As the Father knoweth me, even so know I the Father: and I lay down my life for the sheep.

The deacon/pastor relationship

It is of value to note that preachers are human and have needs. They experience loneliness, isolation, unexpected hostility, a sense of failure and inadequacy, job insecurity, and role confusion. Pastors need emotional support. As human beings, they need to be accepted, loved, encouraged, and appreciated. These needs are to be met in an atmosphere of true love. Because the pastor and his family are human, they will not attain perfection. From time to time, the pastor may misspeak while preaching or teaching. He may share the wrong verse or mispronounce a word. His tie may not match his suit. He may need a haircut. Remember, he is human. Putting him and his family in a glass house or on a pedestal, assuming they will never make a mistake, is a foolish notion. Becoming angry with him and his family when they make a simple error is equally foolish.

The relationship of the deacon/pastor begins before the pastor is called to serve a specific church. Paul shares in 1 Thessalonians 5:12-13:

> And we beseech you, brethren, to know them which labour among you, and are over you in the Lord, and admonish you; and to esteem them very highly in love for their work's sake. And be at peace among yourselves.

There is more involved in knowing a pastor than:

1. Where did the pastor attend school and what degrees does he have?
2. Has he ever pastored a church this size?
3. What are his financial requirements?
4. Is he well known within our Convention?
5. Does he support the Baptist Faith and Message?

6. How much financial support did his previous church give to missions?
7. How many did his previous church baptize last year?

What about:
1. Is he saved?
2. Does he preach the truth?
3. Is he a man of strong character?
4. Is he God's man for our church?
5. Does he have the courage needed to lead our church?

The pastor needs to know some things about the deacons before he accepts a church as pastor. He needs to know:

1. Do the deacons perceive themselves as a "governing board," or as servants appointed by the church?
2. Will they support and stand with the pastor:
    *   When the truth is preached?
    *   When changes are suggested?
    *   When the position and honor of the pastor are falsely attacked?
3. Are the deacons faithful in their stewardship of time, talent, and tithe?
4. Are they faithful in their church attendance?
5. Do they share their faith with the lost?
6. Do the deacons encourage other church members to be involved in fulfilling the purpose of the church?

One of the most serious problems in the church today is an absence of pastoral leadership. This is the fault of both the pastor and the deacons of the individual churches affected. Some pastors are hesitant to take the oversight or be the overseer of the church, for fear they will lose their job. Some deacons are reluctant to submit themselves to the leadership of a pastor. In fact, it is very difficult for some deacons, and impossible for other deacons, to submit to pastoral authority. Yet, Paul, speaking of the role of the pastor, shares in Hebrews 13:17, "Obey them that have the rule over you, and submit yourselves: for they watch for your souls, as they that must give account, that they may do it with joy, and not with grief: for that is unprofitable for you."

Many deacons demonstrate an absence of trust in their relationship with their pastor. Some deacons reflect the view, *Yes, the pastor is God's man for this church, but:*

1. I do not like the way he is changing things.
2. I do not like the way he does things.
3. He is too demanding.
4. He is not concerned enough about the elderly or the youth or the sick, etc.

These are legitimate statements of concern made by some deacons, especially when the previous pastor was a tyrant. When a pastor has the attitude, "This is my church and I will do what I want, when I want, with whom I want," he causes serious problems for the church, which can persist for many years after he is gone. Though the pastor is to be the overseer, he has no right to "lord over" his people. The shepherd is to lead his flock not drive them.

Speaking of the pastor, Paul says in 1 Thessalonians 5:13 the church is to ". . . esteem them very highly in love for their work's sake. And be at peace among yourselves." The church is to respect their pastor. However, please note that the pastor has to earn the respect of his people. A pastor earns respect by being a faithful servant of the Lord. He is to know his people. He is to share with them the truth of God's Word. He is to visit them in time of sickness or need, perform their marriages, baptize their children, and bury their dead. In all that he does for his people, he is to do so out of a heart of love. Performing his ministry and working on behalf of his congregation will generate the love and respect of his people. Church members are warned not to cause conflict among themselves, for such conflict would hinder the pastor's work. Paul says, ". . . be at peace among yourselves" (1 Thess. 5:13).

How can the deacon assist his pastor?

The deacon can pray for his pastor and his pastor's family! Not only does God hear our prayers (2 Kings 20:5; 2 Chron. 7:12; Matt. 21:22), but He also is moved to action by our prayers (2 Sam. 21:14, 24:25). Pray for the protection of your pastor as he travels from place to place in his pastoral duties. Pray for your pastor and his family's protection from demonic forces. One fourth of the miracles Jesus performed consisted of casting out demons. Your pastor also must deal with demonic forces. The demons will do all they can to prevent your pastor from being prepared when he stands to preach or teach. They will discourage him, belittle him, defame him, often causing him to want to surrender and leave the ministry. They will come against him and his family, causing conflicts over money and time spent together. The demons will do all they can to find the spiritual weaknesses of your pastor's family and exploit them. They will use envy and jealously, pride and shame, seeking to convince him that God does not love him and his family as much as He does some other preacher and his family. The demons will remind him of his failures and his inability to accomplish all he desires. They will attack him and his family physically, mentally, spiritually, and emotionally.

Pray for your pastor's wife. I believe it is more difficult to be the wife of a pastor than it is to be the pastor. The pastor's wife lives in the shadows. She seldom receives any recognition. She is expected to keep silent when her husband's preaching angers those within the church. The pastor's wife is expected to give up her time with her husband, while others demand he spend time with them. Pray for her spiritual needs. She too is one of his sheep. She also needs to grow and mature in her Christian faith and walk with the Lord. Pray for your pastor's wife, that the Lord will lead her as she serves Christ.

Pray for your pastor's children. It is imperative to remember they are children, just like any other children. Sometimes they misbehave! Sometimes they are just plain bad! Sometimes they are as precious as any child could ever be. Pray that those who become upset and angry with their father will not mistreat his children. Pray that Satan's attacks against their life will not cause them spiritual harm or danger.

Pray with your pastor for special needs in your church. In my first pastorate, at the Angel Grove Baptist Church in Jacksonville, Alabama, there was a deacon by the name of Ed Johnson. Ed was a godly man. I had not been pastor but a few months when Ed came by our home one day. He shared with me his concern for the spiritual condition of our church and the spiritual needs of those within our community. He asked if I would consent to meet with him every Saturday afternoon for prayer, asking God to do a work of renewal in both the church and the community. During the next year, as we met and prayed, God heard and answered our prayers. The church grew from sixty to one hundred twenty in Sunday school attendance. Discipleship Training attendance grew from twenty-five to one hundred. Wednesday evening services grew from fifteen to more than ninety. The church baptized more new believers than were baptized in many previous years. Several men answered the call to preach. All of the church buildings were renovated. God did some wonderful things. Jesus reminds us in Matthew 21:22, "And all things, whatsoever ye shall ask in prayer, believing, ye shall receive."

The deacon can assist his pastor by supporting the truth the pastor preaches or teaches. Jesus reminds us in Luke 17:1 ". . . It is impossible but that offences will come . . ." It is human nature for people to sin.

When they do, and the pastor's message confronts their sinfulness, some may become offended at the pastor and begin to speak out against him. When those offended by the pastor's remarks speak out against him in the presence of a deacon, the deacon should address their error and support the truth the pastor has shared. The deacon must support his pastor in a loving spirit. The purpose of the deacon is to assist the offended individual to understand and acknowledge the truth the pastor shared, in order that their remarks may not injure others in the church.

Another way the deacon can assist the pastor is by confirming his role as the under-shepherd of the church. I have heard a great deal about "the priesthood of the believer" over the years. I am still not sure what that phrase means, but I can tell you one thing it does not mean. It does not mean that every believer can do his own thing, independent of the will of God. Nor does it mean that everyone is to be the spiritual leader of the church. The pastor, not the deacon, is the under-shepherd of the church. The best way deacons can confirm the role of the under-shepherd is through their public relationship with their pastor. The deacon is not to usurp the pastor's authority, nor is he to call his pastor's messages or actions into question in a public forum without a spiritual foundation. No further action should be taken by the deacon until he has shared his intent with the pastor in a private conversation (Matt. 18:15-17).

A pastor in a First Baptist Church in Georgia was preaching a series of sermons on the "Blood." A deacon's wife confronted this pastor's wife in a local grocery store in a very boisterous manner. She said, "Will you tell your husband something from the members of the church?" The pastor's wife, being very suspicious of the expressions and demeanor of the deacon's wife, said, "What do you want me to share with him?" The deacon's wife said, "Tell him we are tired of the blood. If we wanted blood, we would stick a pig!" Numerous times over the years, as an evangelist, I have had preachers tell me that deacons and deacons' wives have told them what they could or could not preach and teach. At a very early age, my mother shared with me Psalms 105:15, "Saying, Touch not mine anointed, and do my prophets no harm." She instilled in me a godly fear to speak against the pastor God had anointed.

The deacon can assist the pastor financially. There may be some pastors who are overpaid, but I do not know who they are. When you consider what the average pastor makes financially, with four years of college, three years of seminary and two additional years for his doctorate, you must conclude they are not in the ministry for the money. Some critics say, "If I only had to work three hours a week, I wouldn't complain about how much I made." These individuals have no concept of the hours a pastor works each week. It is common for a pastor to spend more than thirty to forty hours per week in sermon preparation alone. A good shepherd will spend many hours each week visiting his people, counseling those with marital problems, drug and alcohol problems, doing premarital counseling, visiting hospitals and nursing homes, or shut-ins, visiting local jails, or meeting with committees. Is it any wonder that 90 percent of those who enter the ministry leave before they reach the age of retirement?

In most Southern Baptist churches, a deacon serves as a member of the budget committee. It is in this forum the deacon can share the financial needs of his pastor. The attitude of the budget committee should never be, "How little can we pay our pastor and staff?" but "How much would God have us pay them?" Christians want God's blessings; but some are not willing to give to others as they would have God give to them. Paul reminds us in 1 Timothy 5:18, ". . . The labourer is worthy of his reward." In Luke 6:38, we are told how we are to give: "Give, and it shall be given unto you; good measure, pressed down, and shaken together, and running over, shall men give into your bosom. For with the same measure that ye mete withal it shall be measured to you again."

A deacon approached me one night after a revival service. He said, "Brother Don, you know why this church doesn't give any more money each week than it does?" I said, "No sir, I don't." He said, "Because we have over three hundred thousand dollars in the bank, and the impression is that we don't need any more money." I asked him, "What are you doing to change the situation?" He said, "I am talking with other deacons and members of the church about my concerns. I am telling them God has not called us to hoard money. We should be doing more for missions and for our pastor." There are many churches like this one. Storing up money for tomorrow is admirable, but doing so at the expense of God's anointed is shameful.

At the Second Baptist church in Columbus, Georgia, "High Attendance Days" were special events. When I arrived, the church was averaging ninety in Sunday school. Soon, we were averaging upward of three hundred fifty in Sunday school. On high attendance days, the deacons were very instrumental in encouraging the entire church to become involved in reaching our community. Deacons invited the mayor of the city and the governor. One Sunday morning, there were upward of six hundred for the worship service. It was hard to tell who was more excited: the deacons or their pastor.

Deacons also assist their pastor by supporting him in the various outreach ministries of the church. I was asked to share communion at a local nursing home while serving as pastor of Second Baptist in Columbus, Georgia. When I asked the deacons to assist me in this communion service, one of the older deacons voiced his reluctance. He was prejudiced against the black patients that were in the nursing home. After some discussion, he decided he would go. The director of the nursing home had the patients brought to the dining area. The older deacon was standing next to me. He appeared very nervous. Just as I started the communion service, the director interrupted me, shouting, "Wait a minute Pastor Ledbetter, I forgot someone!" In a moment, she returned with a young black woman, who had had no arms and the most sever cleft-palate I have ever seen. She positioned the woman in front of the older deacon and informed him how much this woman had looked forward to this service. She then told him how careful he would have to be with her, lest she choke. The director looked at me and said, "He can do it, can't he?" I said, "Sure he can."

When it came time to share the bread, you would have thought he was handling an explosive. He was as patient and tender as anyone could be. To prevent the cracker from falling from her mouth, he took his handkerchief and held it over the hole in her face. Tears flowed down the woman's face as she participated. When she had swallowed the cracker, she said, "Thank you! Thank you!" time after time. As he shared the grape juice, he was even more careful. Again, the tears flowed from her face in appreciation for his service. When he turned and looked at me, tears were flowing from his eyes as well. It was a moving experience.

As the next deacon's meeting began, he stood up and began to cry. Through his tears he said, "I want to share something with you men. The other week when Brother Don asked us to go out to the nursing home and share communion, I did not want to go. You know why. I was born in a generation where whites and blacks never mixed. You saw the director bring that black woman and park her in front of me. When I saw her physical condition, I was afraid! I did not believe I would be able to share with her. However, when I gave her the cracker and the juice, and she began to cry and say, "Thank you!" I have never felt closer to God in my life." He broke down and cried. After a few moments, he turned to me and said, "Brother Don, thank you for allowing me to be a part of such a wonderful experience. I am sorry I have felt as I have about Blacks."

The deacons can assist their pastor and his family by celebrating special events in their lives, such as birthdays, anniversaries, and honors and awards they may receive. I was in a church some years ago with a pastor who was very discouraged. He was doing his best to encourage the church to do God's will. He loved his people, and his words and actions demonstrated that fact. One day as we talked, he said, "You know, Brother Don, I have been pastor here for four years. This church has never recognized a single anniversary, birthday, or any other milestone. It makes me wonder how much my family and I are appreciated."

It was a blessing when church members expressed their love for my family while I was in the pastorate. I remember the time when the church gave my wife Linda a birthday party. Someone had brought a very large, beautiful cake. When the candles were lit, those present began to chant, "Speech, speech." It was such a moving experience. Linda just stood and cried. "It's too beautiful to cut," she said. "Cut it!" they cried. As she tried to cut the cake, she discovered it was made of sponge. Everyone laughed! Then they brought out the real cake. She knew they loved her. It is good to be loved!

If the pastor and his wife have small children, give them an occasional night out. Hiring a babysitter is often difficult for many young pastors. Linda and I were blessed to have church members who recognized this need. Occasionally, some of our church members would come by and say, "Will you let the boys come over to our house for awhile? We know you and Linda would like to have time for yourselves." Most pastors and their wives serve the Lord in churches where they have no family members in the area. Consider this during Christmas time and give the pastor and his wife time for shopping and putting Christmas gifts together for their children.

While visiting in the hospital one day, I ran into a pastor friend I had not seen in awhile. "Where have you been?" I asked. He said, "You know I have been the pastor at my church for seven years. In honor of that fact, the church sent me and my wife to Europe for six weeks." Not every church can or will do anything like this for their pastor. However, it would be nice if a church would reward their pastor and his wife for services rendered. Do for them what God would have you do! Let your pastor and his family know you love them.

What is your relation with your pastor?

Do you pray for your pastor? When was the last time you prayed for him on Saturday night that he might preach under the anointing of the Spirit of God on Sunday? Do you pray for his protection against demonic influences? Do you encourage him and his family? Do you respect his position as the under-shepherd? Do you encourage other church members to respect him as the overseer of the church?

What could you do to improve your relationship with your pastor? Knowing what to do and doing it are two different things. If a church is to be what God would have it be, both the pastor and the deacons are to meet the qualifications, understand their role, and do what is required of them out of a heart of love.

I am sure you have heard the statement that says, "If every member of my church were just like me, what kind of church would my church be?" What if every deacon of your church was just like you? Would your church be a church that supports its pastor? Would your church be a church that prays for him and his family? Would your church be a church that would encourage and support the pastor as he preaches and teaches the truth?

What could you and your wife do to improve your relation with your pastor? What could you and your wife do within and without your church that would enhance his ministry? We often assume others know how we feel or think. Let me encourage you to share your positive views about your pastor with others. However, the greatest compliment you can give your pastor is to implement the truths he preaches and teaches from God's Word.

Chapter 5

The Deacon in Relation to Himself

Self-examination is a difficult task, because we have the tendency of judging ourselves from our own perspective. David reminds us that if we are to know the truth about our self, we must allow God to examine us. David says, "Search me, O God, and know my heart: try me, and know my thoughts: And see if there be any wicked way in me, and lead me in the way everlasting" (Ps. 139:23-24). In that God is *omniscient* (all-knowing), *omnipotent* (all-powerful), and *omnipresent* (everywhere at the same time), He is worthy to examine our life. It is imperative that we accept His evaluation of our life and make changes as needed, if we are to profit from His examination.

As you read this last chapter, I want to ask you some probing questions about who you are in relation to yourself, and challenge you to be all you can be for God. You may choose to pray and ask the Lord to help you to determine your strengths and weaknesses in each of the following topics as you read them.

What about your assurance?

Do you have assurance concerning your relationship with Christ? Are you saved and controlled by the Spirit? When Satan attacks your life and seeks to cause doubt in your mind about your relationship with Christ, how refreshing it is to go back across the years and remember the moment you gave your heart to Christ. Becoming a Christian has been the greatest experience I have ever had in my life! Take a moment and go back in your mind to that place where you accepted Christ. Remember the experience? Remember how wonderful you felt when Christ forgave your sin and gave you the assurance that you were saved? If you have never been saved, you need to address your need for Christ. Confess your sin and invite Christ into your heart. Ask Him to forgive you and save you! If you are a Christian, but you are living in a state of carnality, you need to ask Christ to forgive and restore you, and then begin to live as Christ would have you live.

The old statement, "No one is perfect," is true. There are no perfect Christians. We have all sinned and fallen far short of what we could have done for Christ. We have failed Him in more ways than we can remember. Yet, He loves us! One night, during an invitation, a woman came to me and said, "Brother Don, I am miserable! I am trying my best to be what Christ would have me be. Yet, I fail Him day after day." Throughout her conversation, she used the word "trying" over and over as she shared with me of her effort to appease God. Under the leadership of the Holy Spirit, I felt impressed to share with her a significant thought. I asked her, "Have you ever considered that God doesn't want you to 'try' to be a Christian? God wants you to die! It is only when we die to our self and allow Christ to live through us that we can live the Christian life."

Galatians 2:20 is my favorite verse of Scripture. Listen carefully to what Paul says: "I am crucified with Christ: nevertheless I live; yet not I, but Christ liveth in me: and the life which I now live in the flesh I live by the faith of the Son of God, who loved me, and gave himself for me." Watch this carefully, Paul is saying,

- "I am crucified with Christ . . ." (I am dead.)
- ". . . nevertheless I live . . ." (Yet I am alive.)
- ". . . but Christ liveth in me . . ." (But it is not me that is doing the living.)
- For ". . . the life which I now live in the flesh I live by the faith of the Son of God, who loved me, and gave himself for me." (I am depending on faith—but not my faith.)

Paul says that he is not dependent upon his frail faith to accomplish God's will, but on God's faith in His Son, who dwells within. In that Christ has all power in heaven and earth (Matt. 28:18) and in Him dwells the "fulness of the Godhead" (Col. 2:9), we too can say with Paul, "I can do all things through Christ which strengtheneth me" (Phil. 4:13).

175

Are you sure you were called to be a deacon? The assurance of one's calling is essential to a successful ministry, whether it be as pastor or a deacon. Peter addresses this fact in 2 Peter 1:10 by saying, "Wherefore the rather, brethren, give diligence to make your calling and election sure: for if ye do these things, ye shall never fall." A deacon must have the assurance God has called him to serve as a deacon.

God extends His call to men to become a deacon in various ways. With reference to the first deacons, God used the church to call them to their ministry. How did he call you? Did He call you through a sermon? Did He speak to you about being a deacon through an individual? It is important that we remember from time to time our salvation experience and when the Lord called us to service. Satan will do all he can to cause doubts in the hearts of those who serve Christ. One of Satan's most effective ways of hindering those in church leadership positions is causing them to doubt their salvation and their calling.

The assurance we need concerning our calling sometimes comes through a word of encouragement from someone we believe to be spiritually sound. In Colossians 4:12, Paul shares a word of encouragement with the saints in the Colossian church: "Epaphras, who is one of you, a servant of Christ, saluteth you, always labouring fervently for you in prayers, that ye may stand perfect and complete in all the will of God." What a blessing it is to have a strong Christian we admire share with us an encouraging word about our ministry. Listen to what Paul says to the Christians in the church at Philippi. He says, "Being confident of this very thing, that he which hath begun a good work in you will perform it until the day of Jesus Christ" (Phil. 1:6). Paul is reminding these Christians to remain firm in their faith and allow the Lord to do through them what God wants accomplished.

Are you sure you are in the right church? To be an effective deacon, you must have the assurance that you are in the right church. The "right church" is a church where the Word of God is preached and taught faithfully. It is a church involved in missions, seeking to minister to the needs of the less fortunate within the community, the state, and around the world. It is a church compassionate about winning the lost and discipling new converts. The right church is a church where God would have you and your family place your membership and serve Him faithfully.

Several years ago, I conducted an Associational-wide deacons' retreat in a church in South Carolina. The pastor of that church expressed a liberal bias concerning the Word of God. In a conversation one morning of the retreat, he told me he was disappointed in the "conservative movement" within the Southern Baptist Convention. He believed women should be ordained as deacons and pastors. We had an in-depth discussion on these and other subjects. I am sure he was not impressed with what I shared with him.

Several weeks later, one of the deacons of that church called me. He said, "Brother Don, thank you for coming to our Associational Deacons' Retreat and sharing the truth with us. I must tell you: you are not popular with our pastor and several of the deacons in our church." When I asked him what he meant by this, he said, "We have three or four strong-willed deacons who believe they are to be a 'governing body.' They did not like what you had to say about them being 'servants of the church.' Nor did they appreciate what you had to say about drinking. I was surprised they were back on Saturday and remained for all three sessions. They seldom attend church, but they are faithful to the deacons' meetings. Our pastor thought you were narrow-minded and too old-fashioned. However, he had no comment when someone asked him about the fact that what you shared with us was backed up with Scripture."

I asked this deacon how long he had been a member of his church. When he said he and his family had been there for six or seven years, I was surprised. I told him, I would not raise my family in a church where the pastor did not believe the Bible and did not preach and teach the truth it proclaimed. For a church to be right, the leadership must be right.

Does the Holy Spirit control you?

In Romans 8:5, Paul draws a sharp contrast between those who are without Christ and those who know Christ as their Savior: "For they that are after the flesh do mind the things of the flesh; but they that are after the Spirit the things of the Spirit." It must be understood: it is one thing for the Christian to have the Spirit and quite another for the Spirit to "have" or control the Christian. In this verse, Paul is challenging the Christian to examine his life and determine who is in control—the flesh or the Spirit. Who is in control of your life?

In Romans 8:9, Paul states that the believer has the Spirit, and the Spirit indwells the believer. Some, however, would have us believe that each believer is controlled by the Spirit (Rom. 8:10). "And if Christ be in you, the body is dead because of sin; but the Spirit is life because of righteousness" (Rom. 8:10). If every Christian is controlled by the Spirit, then what is to be said of the *carnal Christian?* In 1 Corinthians 3:1, Paul associates the term *brethren* to the carnal Christian. This is a term he often associates to Christians. Yet, he says that the *carnal Christians* are as babes in Christ, unable to eat the meat of the word, controlled by envy and strife and divisions and not walking in the Spirit (1 Cor. 3:1-5). Paul's remarks clearly indicate that though the carnal Christian has the Spirit of God within him, he is not controlled by the Spirit.

I believe the Bible teaches that when one becomes a Christian he receives the Spirit, and from that moment on, the Spirit indwells his life. Listen to what Paul says in Ephesians 1:13: ". . . after that ye heard the word of truth, the gospel of your salvation: in whom also after that ye believed , ye were sealed with that holy Spirit of promise." I also believe the Bible teaches that a Christian can and often does refuse to allow the Spirit to control his life. This is why Paul says in Ephesians 4:30, "And grieve not the holy Spirit of God, whereby ye are sealed unto the day of redemption." If the Spirit is in total control of the believer, how is it possible for the believer to grieve or sadden the Spirit? The believer has a choice in surrendering himself to the control of the Spirit. As we have noted in the parable of the vine, it is possible for a believer not to be able to bear spiritual fruit, if he does not allow the Holy Spirit to control his life. Jesus says, "Abide in me, and I in you. As the branch cannot bear fruit of itself, except it abide in the vine; no more can ye, except ye abide in me" (John 15:4).

It is important for one's thought life to be controlled by the Spirit. You will not become what you cannot perceive. This does not mean, "If you can perceive it, you will receive it!" It means that what you desire to become in life requires that you envision yourself becoming it. It is only when you know what you would like to achieve that you can formulate a plan that will ensure your objective. Thoughts lead to action! To implement what you desire to become also takes hard work. When the believer is living under the control of the Spirit, the Spirit will lead in the thought process, formulate the plan, and give strength and guidance to accomplish the task.

Before Jesus went back to heaven, He promised He would give His followers the gift of the Holy Spirit. Examine what Jesus says in John 16:13-15.

Howbeit when he, the Spirit of truth, is come, he will guide you into all truth: for he shall not speak of himself; but whatsoever he shall hear, that shall he speak: and he will shew you things to come. He shall glorify me: for he shall receive of mine, and shall shew it unto you. All things that the Father hath are mine: therefore said I, that he shall take of mine, and shall shew it unto you.

As we have already noted, there are three qualifications necessary for the Christian to be controlled by the Spirit. One must desire to be controlled by the Spirit, be willing to deal with any known sin in their life, and ask to be controlled by the Spirit. When one is controlled by the Spirit, he has access to the fullness of Christ; His wisdom, His power, His guidance, His comfort, and all that Christ is becomes available to the Christian through the indwelling Spirit. When you consider what the Spirit can do in and through the life of the Christian, it would appear every Christian would desire to be controlled by the Spirit. However, this is not the case. Consequently, individual Christians and churches are far less than what they could be, because they are not walking in the Spirit. Listen to what Paul says about walking in the Spirit in Galatians 5:16-26.

This I say then, Walk in the Spirit, and ye shall not fulfill the lust of the flesh. For the flesh lusteth against the Spirit, and the Spirit against the flesh: and these are contrary the one to the other: so that ye cannot do the things that ye would. But if ye be led of the Spirit, ye are not under the law. Now the works of the flesh are manifest, which are these; Adultery, fornication, uncleaness, lasciviousness, idolatry, witchcraft, hatred, variance, emulations, wrath, strife, seditions, heresies, envyings, murders, drunkenness, revellings, and such like: of the which I tell you before, as I have also told you in time past, that they which do such things shall not inherit the kingdom of God. But the fruit of the Spirit is love, joy, peace, longsuffering, gentleness, goodness, faith, meekness, temperance: against such there is no law. And they that are Christ's have crucified the flesh with the affections and lusts. If we live in the Spirit, let us also walk in the Spirit. Let us not be desirous of vain glory, provoking one another, envying one another.

In asking to be controlled by the Spirit, the Christian must do so by faith. The author of Hebrews reminds us, "But without faith it is impossible to please him: for he that cometh to God must believe that he is, and that he is a rewarder of them that diligently seek him" (Heb. 11:6). The degree to which a Christian lives the Spirit-filled life depends upon the extent to which he trusts the Lord with every detail of his life. God will not force Himself upon us. We must ask to be controlled by His Spirit. Jesus says in Matthew 7:7, "Ask, and it shall be given you; seek, and ye shall find; knock, and it shall be opened unto you."

Paul further challenges the Christian regarding his relationship to the Spirit and reminds the Christian that we are obligated to give God our very best effort in service to Him.

But if the Spirit of him that raised up Jesus from the dead dwell in you, he that raised up

Christ from the dead shall also quicken your mortal bodies by his Spirit that dwelleth in you. Therefore, brethren, we are debtors, not to the flesh, to live after the flesh. For if ye live after the flesh, ye shall die: but if ye through the Spirit do mortify the deeds of the body, ye shall live. For as many as are led by the Spirit of God, they are the sons of God.

—Romans 8:11-14

Take a moment and ask the Lord to help you examine your life in relation to the Spirit's control. Are there areas in your life that are controlled by the flesh? Ask the Lord to give you guidance to correct these areas. Isn't it a wonderful feeling to be encouraged by the Spirit, when He reveals those areas of our life to us that are pleasing in God's sight? Take a moment and thank Him for His encouragement!

Do you study your Bible, as you should?

A wise person makes time to study what is beneficial to him. When you consider who wrote the Bible and how it came about, you must conclude it is worthy of study. Paul tells us that God is the author of the Bible and the purpose for the Bible to lead man to salvation and help him become spiritually strong: "All scripture is given by inspiration of God, and is profitable for doctrine, for reproof, for correction, for instruction in righteousness" (2 Tim. 3:16). God used forty men over a period of fifteen hundred years to formulate the Bible. These men were comprised of David, a king; Amos a shepherd; Isaiah, a man of royal descent; Peter, a fisherman; James and Jude, two half-brothers of Jesus; and Paul, a tentmaker, to name a few. With rare exception, they did not know each other or the others' writings. Yet, the Bible is marked by a cohesiveness that is astonishing. The wisdom contained within the Bible reveals that its author is all-wise, knowing the end of all things before the beginning. This Bible is the inspired, infallible, and inerrant Word of God.

There are sixty-six books in the Bible, thirty-nine in the Old Testament and twenty-seven in the New Testament. It is of interest to note that the shortest chapter in the Bible is Psalms 117, the longest chapter is Psalms 119, and the middle chapter of the Bible is Psalms 118. There are 594 chapters in the Bible prior to Psalms 118, and 594 chapters in the Bible following Psalms 118. The combined number of chapters in the Bible equal 1,188. The verse that holds the distinction of being the central verse of the Bible is Psalms 118:8. Coincidental? I don't think so! I believe it is just another way that God has of saying, "I put the Bible together!"

I have heard some say, "I don't have time for Bible study." Others have shared with me, "I don't understand the Bible." I have discovered that people make time for what they are interested in and want to do. It is also important to note that the Bible is written to Christians. Therefore, you must be a Christian to understand the teachings of the Bible. Paul reminds us in 1 Corinthians 2:14, "But the natural man [the unsaved person] receiveth not the things of the Spirit of God: for they are foolishness unto him:

neither can he know them, because they are spiritually discerned." The carnal Christian also will have difficulty is studying the Bible, for Paul tells us in 1 Corinthians 3:1-3 that the carnal Christian is childish in his relationship to Christ.

To study the Bible effectively, you must have a desire to know the truths the Bible proclaims. In 1 Peter 2:2-3, Peter reminds us that new Christians have a desire to study the Bible, realizing it is their path to spiritual maturity and discovering God to be worthy of study. Peter says, "As newborn babes, desire the sincere milk of the word, that ye may grow thereby: If so be ye have tasted that the Lord is gracious." The sad truth is that many Christians lose their desire to know God's Word and consequently drift away from God's truths. I remember when I came to know the Lord. I would lie awake at night and listen to preachers on the radio stations out of New Orleans, Louisiana, and Cincinnati, Ohio. You could receive these stations only late at night in North Alabama. I had a desire to know more about the Lord, and those preachers thrilled my soul. Can you remember how hungry you were for the gospel when you first became a Christian?

Biblical knowledge does not come easy. It involves many hours of study. Solomon says in Proverbs 2:1-5:

My son, if thou wilt receive my words, and hide my commandments with thee; so that thou incline thine ear unto wisdom, and apply thine heart to understanding; yea, if thou criest

185

after knowledge, and liftest up thy voice for understanding; if thou seekest her as silver, and searchest for her as for hid treasures; then shalt thou understand the fear of the LORD, and find the knowledge of God.

Do you have a schedule for studying the Bible? Permit me to offer you some suggestions that may assist you in Bible study. First, it is good to have a set time to study your Bible. As you and I both know, scheduling time for anything is difficult. It seems that every hour of the day is already designated for something or someone. Yet, it is important that you choose a time for Bible study and give that time your priority. Second, choose a place for Bible study. Choosing a place for Bible study is as important as choosing a time. If you are fortunate enough to have an office at home, you may want to choose that room. Wherever you choose, it should be a quiet place, well-lit, with room enough for addition study material, a pen and tablet. Third, choose your subject or subjects to study by topic, theme, or text. Before you consider what others have to say about what you are studying, find out all you can on your own from the Bible. Fourth, secure a good Bible concordance and Bible dictionary. Knowing the Hebrew and Greek translation of words and the meaning of events is very important to understanding Scripture. You also may choose to study from several versions of the Bible. Fifth, as you read—read praying—ask God for His guidance and instructions. Ask Him why a verse or text is important to the meaning of a subject. Sixth, write down your thoughts and questions. Take your thoughts and questions back to the Bible and explore them carefully. Seventh, when you have thoroughly explored your topic, consider what others have to say about the subject. Secure books from reputable authors, who have written on the subject you are studying. Eight, you will do well to secure some good Bible commentaries. Commentaries will provide you with an in-depth view of what biblical scholars have learned from the subject you are studying. Ninth, memorize the Scripture! David says, "Thy word have I hid in mine heart, that I might not sin against thee" (Ps. 119:11). Tenth, above all, put what you have learned into practice.

One should not study the Bible just to obtain information. It is necessary to implement the truths you learn from the Bible as you learn them. A deacon who knows God's Word will be better prepared to accomplish his task as a deacon. He will be a better husband and father. He will be able to guide and lead his family through the difficulties of life. He will be able to encourage his family and those within his church who observe his lifestyle. As he anchors himself on God's Word and implements it's truths through his life, day by day, he will allow others to see and know what it means to live by faith and not by sight. Paul says in 1 Corinthians 14:20, "Brethren, be not children in understanding: howbeit in malice be ye children, but in understanding be men."

Let me also encourage you, as a deacon, to involve your family in studying the Bible. Encourage your children to have their own special time for Bible study. You also may choose to study the Bible collectively as a family. Select a special time during the week where you as a family can study God's Word together. Your format may consist of questions and answers about a certain subject. It may be that you or your wife lead the study in certain topics. It may be that the children are given the opportunity to suggest the topic or lead the study. Whatever your format, consider the value that Bible study has for your family and provide it for them.

What about your prayer life?

From the time man first began to pray, the purpose for prayer was made clear. ". . . Then began men to call upon the name of the Lord" (Gen. 4:26). Prayer is the primary means of communicating with God. As you trace man's prayers across the pages of the Bible, you will note the effectiveness of prayer. Consider the following passages of Scripture:

> I called upon the LORD in distress: the LORD answered me, and set me in a large place.
> The LORD is on my side; I will not fear: what can man do unto me?
> —Psalms 118:5-6

> In the day when I cried thou answeredst me, and strengthenedst me with strength in my soul.
> —Psalms 138:3

Then shalt thou call, and the LORD shall answer; thou shalt cry, and he shall say, Here I am. If thou take away from the midst of thee the yoke, the putting forth of the finger, and speaking vanity; and if thou draw out thy soul to the hungry, and satisfy the afflicted soul; then shall thy light rise in obscurity, and thy darkness be as the noon day: And the LORD shall guide thee continually, and satisfy thy soul in drought, and make fat thy bones: and thou shalt be like a watered garden, and like a spring of water, whose waters fail not.

—Isaiah 58:9-11

And while I was speaking, and praying, and confessing my sin and the sin of my people Israel, and presenting my supplication before the LORD my God for the holy mountain of my God; yea, whiles I was speaking in prayer, even the man Gabriel, whom I had seen in the vision as the beginning, being caused to fly swiftly, touched me about the time of the evening oblation. And he informed me, and talked with me, and said, O Daniel, I am now come forth to give thee skill and under-standing. At the beginning of thy supplica-tions the commandment came forth, and I am come to shew thee; for thou art greatly beloved: therefore understand the matter, and consider the vision. [God reveals the vision to Daniel in verses 24-27.]

—Daniel 9:20-23

Be careful for nothing; but in every thing by prayer and supplication with thanksgiving let your requests be made known unto God. And the peace of God, which passeth all understanding, shall keep your hearts and minds through Christ Jesus.

—Philippians 4:6-7

The prayers of Paul reveal his understanding of the effectiveness of prayer and his deep desire for the spiritual growth of his people. Listen to his prayer for the members of the church at Ephesus (Eph. 1:15-23).

Wherefore I also, after I heard of your faith in the Lord Jesus, and love unto all the saints, cease not to give thanks for you, making mention of you in my prayers; that the God of our Lord Jesus Christ, the Father of glory, may give unto you the spirit of wisdom and revelation in the knowledge of him: They eyes of your understanding being enlightened; that ye may know what is the hope of his calling, and what the riches of the glory of his inheritance in the saints, and what is the exceeding greatness of his power to us-ward who believe, according to the working of his mighty power, which he wrought in Christ, when he raised him from the dead, and set him at his own right hand in the heavenly places, far above all principality, and power, and might, and dominion,

and every name that is named, not only in
this world, but also in that which is to come:
And hath put all things under his feet, and
gave him to be the head over all things to the
church, which is his body, the fulness of him
that filleth all in all.

Considering the value of prayer, is it any wonder
that the disciples of Jesus asked Him to teach them
how to pray? Luke records this event in Luke 11:1-4:

And it came to pass, that, as he was praying
in a certain place, when he ceased, one of his
disciples said unto him, Lord, teach us to pray,
as John also taught his disciples. And he said
unto them, When you pray, say, Our Father
which art in heaven, Hallowed be thy name,
Thy kingdom come. Thy will be done, as in
heaven, so in earth. Give us day by day our
daily bread. And forgive us our sins; for we
also forgive every one that is indebted to us.
And lead us not into temptation; but deliver
us from evil.

Though this is often referred to as "The Lord's
Prayer," it would be more accurate to say it is a
model prayer.

There are some very important truths contained
within this prayer that will enhance our prayer life.
First, it is of value to note the *person* to whom our
prayers are to be addressed— *"Our Father"* (Luke
11:2). As Christians, we have been adopted into

the family of God. Paul tells us that God has ". . . predestinated us unto the adoption of children by Jesus Christ to himself, according to the good pleasure of his will" (Eph. 1:5). When we become the children of God, He becomes our Father and begins to mold us into His own image. Isaiah says, "But now, O LORD, thou art our father; we are the clay, and thou our potter; and we all are the work of thy hand" (Isa. 64:8). As a father, God instructs his children (Deut. 4:36); He corrects them (Prov. 3:12); He provides for them (Acts 17:25); and He protects them (Rom. 8:31). Knowing He wants nothing but the best for us, we should go to Him with our needs and our praise for His goodness to us.

Second, Jesus reminds us of the *position* of the One to whom we pray—Our Father *"which art in heaven"* (Luke 11:2). God is exalted! He is above all! Moses said of God in Deuteronomy 4:39, "Know therefore this day, and consider it in thine heart, that the LORD he is God in heaven above, and upon the earth beneath: there is none else." In Deuteronomy 33:26, Moses adds, "There is none like unto the God of Jeshurun, who rideth upon the heaven in thy help, and in his excellency on the sky." Samuel says of God, "There is none holy as the LORD: for there is none beside thee: neither is there any rock like our God" (1 Sam. 2:2). In that our God is above all gods and exalted above all things, there is nothing He does not know or cannot do. He is worthy of our petitions.

Third, Jesus reminds us of the *holiness* of the One to whom we pray— *"hallowed be thy name"* (Luke 11:2). God is holy, and we are to reverence His holiness! He is perfect in every aspect and always true to His nature. Listen to Psalms 99: 1-5: "The LORD reigneth; let the people tremble: he sitteth between the cherubims; let the earth be moved. The LORD is great in Zion; and he is high above all the people. Let them praise thy great and terrible name; for it is holy. The king's strength also loveth judgment; thou dost establish equity, thou executest judgment and righteousness in Jacob. Exalt ye the LORD our God, and worship at his footstool; for he is holy." When we go to Him in prayer, we can trust His judgment and rely on His goodness and fairness. Solomon says, "Every word of God is pure: he is a shield unto them that put their trust in him" (Prov. 30:5).

Fourth, as we go to God in prayer, we should pray that His will becomes a part of our daily life— *"thy will be done, as in heaven, so in earth"* (Luke 11:2). God's will for man is in correlation to man's acceptance of God's Christ and his daily yielding of self to Christ. John says in 1 John 4:10, "Herein is love, not that we loved God, but that he loved us, and sent his Son to be the propitiation for our sins." Peter reminds us that we can rely upon God's will being accomplished, for "The Lord is not slack concerning his promise, as some men count slackness; but is longsuffering to us-ward, not willing than any should perish, but that all should come to repentance" (2 Pet. 3:9). As God's child, we have the privilege of sharing God's will with others, that they may become a part of His kingdom. Jesus says, ". . . ye shall receive power, after that the Holy Ghost is come upon you: and ye shall be witnesses unto me both in Jerusalem, and in all Judaea, and in Samaria, and unto the uttermost part of the earth" (Acts 1:8). As you pray, ask God to help you do His will.

There are two phases to the "model" prayer. The first phase speaks of the One to whom we pray, and the second phase speaks of four things for which we are to pray. First, we are to ask God for our daily needs— *"Give us day by day our daily bread"* (Luke 11:3). Each morning, I begin my day asking God to supply my needs for the day—spiritually, physically, mentally, and emotionally. We have His promise in Matthew 21:22: "And all things, whatsoever ye shall ask in prayer, believing, ye shall receive." I heard of an older deacon who said, "Every morning when I get out of bed, I get down on my knees and go back across the years in my mind to Calvary. I envision Christ on the cross. I see Him dying for me. I see Him removed from the cross and buried in a borrowed tomb. I envision His resurrection, His return back to heaven, and the coming of the Holy Spirit to live in my life. Then I pray for God's Spirit to direct my path as I begin the day. I rise and begin my day, realizing what Christ has done for me, knowing He loves me and dwells within me. With such knowledge, I am able to face the day with the confidence: 'I can do all things through Christ which strengtheneth me'" (Phil. 4:13).

Second, our prayers should demonstrate a desire for forgiveness for our sins, and our willingness to forgive those who have wronged us— *"And forgive us our sins; for we also forgive every one that is indebted to us"* (Luke 11:4). Confession of sins is not an easy task. Our pride and self-interest often clouds our understanding of what is truth. If we ask God to share with us the truths we need to face our sins, He will enable us to understand our spiritual condition through the ministry of the indwelling Spirit. In John 16: 8-15, Jesus says,

> And when he is come, he will reprove the world of sin, and of righteousness, and of judgment: Of sin, because they believe not on me; of righteousness, because I go to my Father, and ye see me no more; of judgment, because the prince of this world is judged. I have yet many things to say unto you, but ye cannot bear them now. Howbeit when he, the Spirit of truth, is come, he will guide you into all truth: for he shall not speak of himself; but whatsoever he shall hear, that shall he speak: and he will shew you things to come. He shall glorify me: for shall receive of mine, and shall shew it unto you. All things that the Father hath are mine: therefore said I, that he shall take of mine, and shall shew it unto you.

Paul tells us that those who pray for forgiveness are blessed. ". . . Blessed are they whose iniquities are forgiven, and whose sins are covered" (Rom. 4:7). In Ephesians 4:32, Paul tells us why we should have a forgiving spirit toward those who have wronged us: "And be ye kind one to another, tenderhearted, forgiving one another, even as God for Christ's sake hath forgiven you." Paul simply reminds us that if

God can forgive us of all we have done against Him, surely we should be willing to forgive those who have wronged us. If we are unwilling to forgive others and expect God to forgive us, what does that say about us? Are there sins in your life that you should confess? Is there someone you need to forgive?

Third, we should ask God for strength and guidance in order that we will not be led into temptation—*"And lead us not into temptation"* (Luke 11:4). Temptation to sin is a daily occurrence in the life of the believer. Satan will do everything he can to cause the Christian to fail. Jesus identifies Satan as the "tempter" in Matthew 4:3, as Satan sought to tempt Jesus in the wilderness. It must be understood that God does not tempt us. "Let no man say when he is tempted, I am tempted of God: for God cannot be tempted with evil, neither tempteth he any man" (James 1:13). As we pray, we need to ask God for His wisdom and strength to lead us when Satan seeks to tempt us. We need to ask God to help us to "Put on the whole armour of God, that [we] may be able to stand against the wiles of the devil" (Eph. 6:11).

Is being tempted a sin? Satan will make you think it is! The truth is that even the strongest Christians are tempted from time to time. When this occurs, it is good to remember what Paul says: "There hath no temptation taken you but such as is common to man: but God is faithful, who will not suffer you to be tempted above that ye are able; but will with the temptation also make a way to escape, that ye may be able to bear it" (1 Cor. 10:13). It also must be understood we are not perfect and from time to time, we yield to Satan's temptations. A Christian is not exempt from sin. Satan tempts us; then he taunts us. He will do all he can to cause the Christian to yield to sin. When the Christian sins, he will seek to make them believe there is no hope of recovery. He tells the guilty Christian how bad they are, that God doesn't love them and won't help them. We need to remember that Satan ". . . is a liar, and the father of it" (John 8:44). God does love us and He continues to forgive us of sins. Paul reminds us that God not only has accepted us through the blood of Christ, but He provides for us the forgiveness of sins according to the riches of His grace (Eph. 1:6-7).

Fourth, we are instructed to pray for deliverance from evil— ". . . *But deliver us from evil*" (Luke 11:4). Literally from "Satan," the evil one. Satan is the source of evil in this world. Satan is behind the deaths caused by abortion and sexually transmitted diseases. He rules in the hearts of the world's dictators, who cause their people misery, hardship, and death. He guides the politicians, who favor power over being servants for the good of those who elected them. He shrouds God's truth and distorts the hearts of homosexuals, enabling them to believe a lie (Rom. 1:28). He fills the heart of preachers with fear, preventing them from preaching God's Word, thus causing nations to turn away from God's truths and embrace Satan's lies (Lam. 4:13). Jesus describes Satan as "The thief [who] cometh not, but for to steal, and to kill, and to destroy . . ." (John 10:10). In John 8:44, Jesus says of Satan, ". . . He was a murderer from the beginning, and abode not in the truth, because there is no truth in him. When he speaketh a lie, he speaketh of his own: for he is a liar, and the father of it." In that God alone can overpower Satan, we need to pray for deliverance from Satan's power and influence in our lives and in our world.

We need to take a look at what is going on behind the scenes and carefully examine the corruption that is taking place in this world. The church and the Christian are under attack today as never before. John says that Satan is the accuser of the brethren before God day and night (Rev. 12:10). As mortals, we don't have the power or ability to combat Satan on our own. We need to be protected from Satan's power. We need God! David says, "For the LORD God is a sun and shield: the LORD will give grace and glory: no good thing will he withhold from them that walk uprightly" (Ps. 84:11). When we pray, we need to ask God to help us take ". . . the shield of faith, wherewith [we] shall be able to quench all the fiery darts of the wicked [one]" (Eph. 6:16).

Are you praying as you should? You may wish to write out your prayer requests. Keeping a record of your prayers will enrich your prayer life. In times of spiritual fatigue and demonic conflict, the assurance of answered prayers will serve as a great source of encouragement. Listen to David in Psalms 63:1-7, when he was experiencing persecution in his life. Having escaped into the wilderness, he reflected upon God's goodness and the answers he had received from his prayers.

O God, thou art my God; early will I seek thee:
my soul thirsteth for thee, my flesh longeth
for thee in a dry and thirsty land, where no
water is; to see thy power and thy glory, so
as I have seen thee in the sanctuary. Because
thy lovingkindness is better than life, my lips
shall praise thee. Thus will I bless thee while
I live: I will lift up my hands in thy name.
My soul shall be satisfied as with marrow and
fatness; and my mouth shall praise thee with
joyful lips: When I remember thee upon my
bed, and meditate on thee in the night watches.
Because thou hast been my help, therefore in
the shadow of thy wings will I rejoice.

A wise man closes his day in reflection of how
he spent his day for God. It is a wiser man who
closes his day in communion with God through
prayer. Prayer affords us the opportunity to recreate
the events of the day and to express our appreciation
to God for His goodness. Prayer enables us to see
our life from God's perspective. It affords answers
to life's problems and gives us directions to fulfill
His will. Prayer brings comfort to the brokenhearted
and healing to the sick. There is no greater blessing
given to the Christian than the privilege of prayer.
How fitting it is for the Christian to close his day in
prayer with God.

Are you committed to winning souls?

Solomon says, "The fruit of the righteous is
a tree of life; and he that winneth souls is wise"

(Prov. 11:30). Personal soul winning should be a primary responsibility of every deacon. Being right with Christ is required to be a soul winner, but just living right will not of itself win anyone to Christ. Are you winning others to Christ? Does the way you live make sinners say, "I don't know what that man has, but he has something I want"? To win them to Christ, you must tell them what is involved in being a Christian. Less we forget, Paul reminds us, in Romans 10:17, ". . . faith cometh by hearing, and hearing by the word of God." Paul also tells us:

> That if thou shalt confess with thy mouth the Lord Jesus, and shalt believe in thine heart that God hath raised him from the dead, thou shalt be saved. For with the heart man believeth unto righteousness; and with the mouth confession is made unto salvation. . . . For whosoever shall call upon the name of the Lord shall be saved.
>
> —Romans 10:9-10, 13

Are you looking for an example to help you become a better soul-winner? Consider Jesus! Jesus says in Mark 1:17, ". . . Come ye after me, and I will make you to become fishers of men." Like Jesus, you must go to where sinners live. "And Jesus went about all the cities and villages . . ." (Matt. 9:35). Like Jesus, you also must have compassion for the lost. "But when he saw the multitudes, he was moved with compassion on them . . ." (Matt. 9:36).

Soul-winning is not easy. To be a soul-winner, you must have a burden for the lost and a desire to see the lost come to know the fullness of Christ, avoid hell, and be assured of heaven. You must love the sinner, be positive in your presentation of the gospel, and have a don't-give-up attitude. You must learn that the same approach of witnessing doesn't work on everyone. Be flexible! You must not be easily offended; realize that it is not you the lost are rejecting, but Christ. Be consistent, truthful, loving, and kind as you share the gospel. Be assured God will bless your efforts!

It is both the responsibility and the privilege of every deacon to encourage the members of their church to become involved in implementing God's purpose for their church. Before Jesus went back to heaven, He shared with His disciples the Great Commission. He said:

> Go ye therefore, and teach all nations, baptizing them in the name of the Father, and of the Son, and of the Holy Ghost: Teaching them to observe all things whatsoever I have commanded you: and, lo, I am with you always, even, unto the end of the world. Amen.
>
> —Matthew 28:19-20

As you examine this passage of Scripture, you will note that the church is to win the sinner, mature the saint, and mirror the Savior. First, the church is to *win the sinner*. Evangelism requires church members to *"go"* beyond the walls of the church to where sinners live. Finding the demographic information for your church's community is easy. Go on the Internet, and you will find a number of demographic sites with the information you will need. You may also contact your local utilities services for demographic information. Once you know whom and how many people live within your community, this information must be assimilated to church members in order to reach these people for Christ.

The Sunday school is the outreach arm of the church. In the average Baptist church, Sunday school will average forty-five to fifty percent in attendance of those enrolled in Sunday school. To increase the Sunday school attendance, a church must increase its Sunday school enrollment and work the enrollment. Just placing people on the Sunday school rolls is not enough. You must contact them, week by week, letting them know they are of value and the members of the church care about them.

Not only does the enrollment of the Sunday school affect church attendance, it also has a direct correlation on souls saved. The Sunday school is the barometer of the church. As the Sunday school goes, so goes the church. As a deacon in your church, you may choose to assist your Sunday school director in gathering and assimilating the demographic information that will help your church reach your community. You may be led of God to start a new Sunday school class and become its teacher. Your participation in reaching the lost in your community should serve as an example for others.

It is the will of God that none ". . . should perish, but that all should come to repentance" (2 Pet. 3:9). Yet, only three out of every one hundred Baptists ever win a soul to Christ. The average Baptist church baptizes less than 10 each year. Did you know that if a church had forty people, twenty teams of two, and each of these twenty teams won one soul every other week to Christ, that church would baptize 520 people in a year? Consider the following:

1. 40 people → 20 teams → 1 soul every 2 weeks = 520 for baptism per year
2. 20 people → 10 teams → 1 soul every 2 weeks = 260 for baptism per year
3. 10 people → 5 teams → 1 soul every 2 weeks = 130 for baptism per year
4. 4 people → 2 teams → 1 soul every 2 weeks = 52 for baptism per year
5. 2 people → 1 team → 1 soul every 2 weeks = 26 for baptism per year

Second, the church is to *mature the saint*—"teach all nations" (Matt. 28:19). In the Sunday school seminar I conduct, I make this statement: "The church that does not have a training program for its members is either dead or dying." Every major company has training programs for its employees; so should the church. Yet, in many of our Southern Baptist churches there are no training programs. If the lost are to be won to Christ, Christians must be trained to win them. It is also imperative to teach new converts the Word of God, that they may be strengthened and better prepared to win their family, friends, and neighbors to Christ. One of the qualifications for a deacon is that he be a man of "wisdom" (Acts 6:3). Solomon reminds us in Proverbs 9:9: "Give instruction to a wise man, and he will be yet wiser: teach a just man, and he will increase in learning." Have you ever wondered what would happen in our churches if every deacon became a soul winner? How many people did you lead to Christ last year?

Third, the purpose of the church is to *mirror* the Savior. *"He is with us always"* (Matt. 28:20). In all that the church does, what it does should be done as unto the Lord (Col. 3:23). We are told that those Christians in Antioch lived so much like Christ that they were ". . . called Christians first in Antioch" (Acts 11:26). As a result of their service for Christ, ". . . much people was added unto the Lord" (Acts 11:24). Likewise, those who live within our church communities need to have Christians who live and act like Christ, love them with the love of Christ, and demonstrate to them Christ's mercy and grace. In mirroring the Savior, the church will demonstrate that ". . . the Son of man is come to seek and to save that which is lost" (Luke 19:10). As a deacon, does your life mirror Christ?

Are you a good steward for Christ?

Stewardship is personal responsibility for taking care of another person's property or financial affairs. Stewardship for the Christian involves the use of time, talents, spiritual gifts, tithes, and offerings. Speaking of the value of time, Solomon says in Ecclesiastes 3:1-8:

To every thing there is a season, and a
time to every purpose under the heaven:
A time to be born, and a time to die; a time
to plant, and a time to pluck up that which is
planted;
A time to kill, and a time to heal; a time to
break down, and a time to build up;
A time to weep, and a time to laugh; a
time to mourn, and a time to dance;
A time to cast away stones, and a time
to gather stones together; a time to embrace,
and a time to refrain from embracing;
A time to get, and a time to lose; a time to
keep, and a time to cast away;
A time to rend, and a time to sew; a time
to keep silence, and a time to speak;
A time to love, and a time to hate; a time
of war, and a time of peace.

A good steward is one who uses his time well.
When I was working on my doctorate degree with
Luther Rice Seminary, I was asked to account for
every minute of each day, for a month. I was amazed
at how much time I wasted. I have learned over the
years that people make time for what they want to
do. How much time do you spend in Bible study,
prayer, soul-winning, and the other things that would
enhance the ministry of your church?

What about the use of your talents and spiritual
gifts? There are similarities and differences between
talents and spiritual gifts. However, both of these are
for the benefit of others. Neither talents nor spiritual

gifts are to be used for selfish purposes. Every person has natural talents, regardless of their spiritual relationship to Christ. However, the Holy Spirit gives the believer spiritual gifts when they accept Christ to be used to advance the kingdom of God (1 Cor. 12:11). What are your talents? Are you using them for God?

What are your spiritual gifts? Spiritual gifts are important to the body of Christ. In fact, they are so important that Paul says, ". . . concerning spiritual gifts, brethren, I would not have you ignorant." Paul proceeds to share that spiritual gifts are used by God to advance His kingdom. Paul identifies spiritual gifts in three passages of Scripture.

In Romans 12
- Prophecy
- Teaching
- Exhortation
- Giving
- Leadership
- Mercy
- Service

In 1 Corinthians 12
- Administration
- Wisdom
- Knowledge
- Faith
- Healing
- The working of miracles
- Prophecy

- The discernment of spirits
- Apostles
- Tongues
- The interpretation of tongues
- Prophets
- Teachers
- Helpers

In Ephesians 4
- Apostles
- Prophets
- Evangelists
- Pastors/teachers

Some would argue there are other spiritual gifts noted in the Bible, and offer "hospitality" (1 Pet. 4:9).

Do you know what your spiritual gift or gifts are? There are tests that you may take to help you determine your spiritual gifting. Ask your pastor if he has access to a test, or you may wish to go to your local Christian bookstore and secure a test. Peter would have us know that it is important that we not only know our spiritual gift or gifts, but also practice them day by day. "As every man hath received the gift, even so minister the same one to another, as good stewards of the manifold grace of God" (1 Pet. 4:10).

Do you tithe? Some would argue that tithing is an Old Testament requirement and has no relevance for today. However, tithing is commended in both the Old Testament (Gen. 14:20) and the New Testament (Matt. 23:23). Most often, when preachers teach on the subject of tithing, they use Malachi 3:8-11. Malachi makes God's view on tithing very clear:

> Will a man rob God? Yet ye have robbed me. But ye say, Wherein have we robbed thee? In tithes and offerings. Ye are cursed with a curse: for ye have robbed me, even this whole nation. Bring ye all the tithes into the storehouse, that there may be meat in mine house, and prove me now herewith, saith the LORD of hosts, if I will not open you the windows of heaven, and pour you out a blessing, that there shall not be room enough to receive it. And I will rebuke the devourer for your sakes, and he shall not destroy the fruits of your ground; neither shall your vine cast her fruit before the time in the field, saith the LORD of hosts.

This passage of Scripture reveals that God not only requires the believer to tithe, but also informs those who do not that they are a thief. God also tells us where the tithe is to be given, to the "storehouse," the church. God says those who do not tithe are "cursed." I don't know about you, but I don't want me or my family cursed by God. Is the amount of money your church receives each year pleasing to God? It is not if you and your family do not give your part. For a Christian not to tithe:
1. Is un-Christian, illogical, and self-condemning
2. Is ungrateful

3. Is arrogant
4. Is hurtful both to you and to others
5. Denies God's judgment (Mal. 3:9)
6. Shows an absence of respect for God

Malachi 3: 8 tells us the believer is to give an offering. This is an amount to be given that is over and above the tithe. We are not told where the offering is to be given or to whom. I believe the offering is the amount God would have the believer give to special needs and events that are used to advance the kingdom. If it were not for Christian friends, who have shared their offerings with my evangelistic ministry, I would not have been able to remain in evangelism. Do you give over and above your tithe? Where and to whom do you share your offerings?

It would do us well to remember that there is no one who wants to bless us more than God does. He has a plan for our life, which includes our finances, and if we do our part, He will bless us beyond measure. To get in on God's plan of financial blessings, you must learn to give. Jesus says in Luke 6:38, "Give, and it shall be given unto you; good measure, pressed down, and shaken together, and running over, shall men give into your bosom. For with the same measure that ye mete withal it shall be measured to you again." I have never met a stingy church or a stingy Christian that were blessed by God!

Who are your friends?

Amos 3:3 asks the question, "Can two walk together, except they be agreed?" The friends you choose are a reflection of who you are, and the people you surround yourself with will define the man whom you will become. It is imperative that you choose your friends wisely. There are two ways to choose your friends. You either choose them based on who you are, or on who you want to be. No matter what aspect of life you are trying to improve, there are those who will help you reach your goal. Change is never easy, and when you begin to change from who you are to who you want to be, some of your friends will do all they can to hold on to the "you" they have known.

Patsy was a narcotics agent for the Atlanta Police Department. When the women of our church started visiting her, she was not excited about what they had to share. As they continued to visit with her, she realized that not only did these women care about her, but also Jesus loved her. Several weeks after she became a Christian, she came into my office crying. She said, "Brother Don, my old friends won't have anything to do with me anymore." I said, "Praise the Lord!" She said, "Oh, Brother Don, they have been my friends for years. Now they don't come by or call." I said, "Praise the Lord!" She said, "Why are you saying that?" I said, "Because the 'old you' died several weeks ago. Your old friends do not know the 'new you.' You have changed, and your old friends do not like the 'new you.'" She said, "I haven't thought about it that way. Praise the Lord!" I challenged her to deal with her old friends with the understanding that she had changed and do her best to win them to Christ.

If you are unwilling to be friendly with those who are lost, what hope do you have of ever winning them to Christ? Examine the life of Jesus and note with whom He associated Himself.

And it came to pass, that as Jesus sat at meat in his house, many publicans and sinners sat also together with Jesus and his disciples: for there were many, and they followed him. And when the scribes and Pharisees saw him eat with publicans and sinners, they said unto his disciples, How is it that he eateth and drinketh with publicans and sinners? When Jesus heard it, he saith unto them, They that are whole have no need of the physician, but they that are sick: I came not to call the righteous, but sinners to repentance.

—Mark 2:15-17

Is there someone un-churched in your neighborhood that you could befriend? Maybe you could invite him to go fishing, hunting, or golfing. Is there an un-churched family you and your wife could invite over for a cook-out? A wise man once said, "A man that hath friends must shew himself friendly . . ." (Prov. 18:24).

As you examine your life, are you pleased with who you are? What does the choice of your friends say about you? Do you believe the friends you have will enable you to become a better Christian? As a friend, what are you doing to help your friends become a Christian or a better Christian?

Are you reading good books?

What books are you reading and why are you reading them? Spiritual leaders need to know many things about advancing the cause of Christ. There are volumes of good books that will provide you with helpful information. Like anything else worthwhile, reading comes with a price. You must find the material you need and commit yourself to the time it takes to read it. Reading should not be for the sole purpose of obtaining knowledge. The knowledge one receives from reading should help others become a better person. The excuses, "I don't have time to read," or "I don't read well," are just that . . . excuses.

Reading books is the key to learning! Reading expands the mind. Over the years, I have had Christians ask me, "How can I know which books will help me grow as a Christian" and "Where can I find the books I need?" I have answered these questions by telling them how I choose books for reading that will help me grow spiritually. First, I seek a book that will help me meet a specific need in my life. However, before I begin to look for a book that deals with this specific topic, I search the Scriptures to find out what God's Word has to say about the matter, and then I begin my search for a book that will provide me with help. I have learned over the years that not all books are worth reading. Some are so full of fluff that they offer no substantive value. The information from some books does not substantiate biblical truths and only causes confusion. This is why it is imperative to know what God says about the topic you are investigating before you choose a book to read.

Where can you find a book that will assist you in your spiritual growth? Ask your pastor or some seasoned Christian friend for their suggestions concerning a book that will be of value to you. Check with your church librarian! Go to your local Christian book store and ask the manager if he/she will offer you their suggestions for a good book.

Second, I choose books to read that will encourage and inspire me. I don't care who we are—all of us need a word of encouragement and a word from God that will inspire us from time to time. I enjoy reading books written about the life histories of great men of God, such as George Muller and Billy Sunday; books of sermons preached by great preachers like Dr. Vance Havner, Dr. George W. Truett, Dr. W. A. Criswell, and Dr. R. G. Lee; and the works of Christian apologetics, such as Dr. Ravi Zacharias. I enjoy reading Christian literature by Dr. Warren Wiersbe and Dr. J. Vernon McGee. I enjoy reading! You may be encouraged and inspired by other books. Yet, I challenge you to find those books that will lift your spirits and will enable you to be a happier, more committed Christian.

Third, I also read books that are designed to help me help others. If I am to give my best self to Christ's service, I need all the help I can get. Reading books, authored by those who have the wisdom and experience I am seeking and designed to help me help others, is worthy of my time and effort. I have spent countless hours over the years reading books on homiletics, how to exegete Scripture, the value of expository preaching, evangelism, soul-winning, and how to give an invitation, all for the purpose of helping me to be a better preacher, soul-winner, and evangelist. I have spent equally as many hours reading books that were designed to help me be a better teacher of God's Word. The information that I have obtained on teaching has helped me in the marriage retreats, deacons' retreats, and Sunday school seminars I conduct.

I also am asked, "How can I obtain the best results from what I read?" As you read, read praying. Remember Jesus said, ". . . when he, the Spirit of truth, is come, he will guide you into all truth . . ." (John 16:13). As you read, ask the Spirit to help you understand and formulate what you are reading. Ask Him to inform you how you can use what you are reading to help grow your spiritual life and the lives of others. It is a good idea to have a pen and tablet near you, in order to write down the information the Spirit gives you as you read.

Here is another question that is worthy of consideration. "What do I do with the information I have obtain when I have finished reading a book?" Make a folder and place all the information you have received from that book in the folder and file it for future reference. The information you will need to place in the folder will consist of the title, author, publisher of the book, and the reason you purchased the book. You also will need to write a paragraph on what you believe the author's purpose for the book was. Make a list of the chapter headings and write a paragraph or two explaining each chapter. You also may want to identify what you believed was the most important chapter in the book and give your reason or reasons why. Now, make a list of how you believe the book can benefit your life and the lives of others. In days to come, you will be able to return to your folder and remember most of the information you received when you first read the book.

My father only had two or three years of formal education. When he came home from the navy after World War Two, he went to work in a local foundry. The amount of money he made never afforded him the opportunity to pay someone for something he could learn to do himself. Not being able to read, he would go to the library and ask the librarian for books that provided pictures illustrating what he wanted to learn to do. When he built our home, he would secure books that had pictures showing how to cut the boards, do the wiring, lay the brick, install the windows and the doors, etc. He did the same with the car! He found books that showed him how to rebuild an engine. He learned by trial and error. He was a quick learner. Over the years, Dad became a good gunsmith, electrician, and woodworker. He learned to make guitars and violins. Many of Dad's guitars and violins are in use in worship for God across America. As Dad learned to do these things, with Mother's help, he learned to read. Before he died, he read the Bible through more than fifty times. How many books have you read since you graduated from high school? What area of your life needs to be enriched by the wisdom you could obtain from books?

How much time do you spend with your family?

A young married couple soon will learn how important time management is for a successful Christian home. To spend quality time with your family, you must schedule your time. Both parents must schedule their time for each other, their children, their church, parents, relatives, friends, jobs, hobbies, sports, and what seems like a thousand other things. Scheduling time can become overwhelming. Yet, the benefits that can be obtained from scheduling time for what is really important are worth the effort. You must learn to establish priorities, deciding what is most important. Some, by the way they live, acknowledge the fact that their job, sports, and hobbies are more important than their family. Whatever receives most of your time will evidence what is most important to you.

In order to assure more time with the family, it is a good idea to have a work schedule for each member of the family to perform household duties. Most women work outside the home. It is not fair for her to have to work outside the home and then be responsible for all the household work. Designate responsibilities for house and yard work for each member of the family. Make a list of who will do what and when. Give the children clear and fair instructions of the consequences, if individual responsibilities are not accomplished. Avoid becoming a perfectionist! In all you do, be consistent! Remember, children learn by example.

Guard your time with your family! Avoid allowing things of lesser importance to upset your scheduled time with your family. You will never have a second chance to relive this day. It is important to remember that as you live this day, you are making memories. In years to come, you will look back and be thankful for the time God gave you with your family and the moments you were able to share with them.

Cherish your time with your family. Live each day as though it might be your last. Some years ago in a revival meeting, a man said, "Brother Don, tomorrow night we will be eating in the fellowship hall before the revival service. After we have eaten, I want you to do me a favor." The next night, after I had finished eating my meal, he came over to me and said. "Are you ready?" I said, "Yes, sir! I am." I didn't know what this man wanted me to do, but I got up and followed him. He took me to the cemetery behind the church. As he opened the gate and started into the cemetery, he took out his handkerchief and began to cry. He walked over to a new grave and stood there for a few moments. Then he said, "Brother Don, I want to introduce you to my wife. My wife and I were married for thirty-eight years. I am a mail carrier in the community and, with rare exception, she rode with me every day. I loved the ground she walked on and she loved me. Back in June she took sick and two weeks later she died. Only God knows how much I miss her." After a few moments, he turned and said, "Do you preach to a lot of people?" When I told him I did, he said, "Will you do me another favor? Will you tell people not to take their mate for granted? One day they will kiss their mate goodbye their last time. Will you tell parents to love their children, for they never know when God may take them away? Will you tell people to love their church, for one day they won't be able to go?" Cherish your time with your family!

What are you doing with your family? How much time do you spend with them each day? When I ask those who attend the marriage retreat I conduct what they remember most about what their parents gave them as a child, the majority respond by saying, "I remember the time they spent with me." What will your children remember about the time you spend with them? Are you putting in the time with your mate and children to let them know they are worth your time? Dad, you need to spend time with your children. If you have more than one child, do things with all of them together. Read them Bible stories. Tell them how it was when you were their age. Build a godly relationship with your children. I also suggest that you take each of your children and spend quality alone time with them. Have a one-on-one experience with each child.

Dad, it is imperative that you both tell and show your family that you love them. Can you remember the last time you put your arms around your wife and children and shared with them how much you love them? When was the last time you brought your wife home some flowers or your children some candy? If your children are grown, when was the last time you called them and told them you love them? When was the last time you planned a special event for your entire family, where all of your family came together and enjoyed some time of love and fellowship?

How much time do you give your family spiritually? Do you pray with them? Do you give your family time to ask you questions about the Bible? The greatest joy of being Christian parents is leading your children to a personal relationship with Christ. Ask your children if there are some things they would like for you to pray about with them. Assure them you are concerned about their spiritual condition. It is important that your family see you reading the Bible and hear you praying. Do not be afraid to express you spiritual concerns with your family. They need to know that you also are maturing as a Christian. There is room for improvement in all our lives.

What is your relationship with your pastor and church staff?

A productive relationship between any two individuals is always a work in progress. How you get along with the pastor and staff at your church depends largely on how you want to get along with them. There is a sincere reluctance by some deacons to get too close to their pastor. The reluctance of some is because of their understanding of the tenure of the pastor. They feel, "The pastor and his family will not be here long. If I get too close to him, it will hurt too much when he leaves." Some are reluctant to get close to their pastor because they have been hurt or offended by a former pastor. Remember: every pastor and his family are human, unique, and subject to likes and dislikes. They too can be offended. They need to know they are loved and appreciated. They, too, need to be shepherded from time to time.

Relationships must be built! Permit me to suggest several ways you can build a positive relationship with your pastor and staff. First, you begin with a desire that in all you do, your relationship with them will magnify the Lord. This means you will treat others as you would have them treat you. Second, you should look for ways you can support their ministry positively. You may want to join the choir or teach a class or become a part of a visiting team. Being present for all the worship services will show support to and for your pastor. Third, you should show genuine interest in them as individuals and what they are doing for Christ through the church. Find out their likes and dislikes. Seek to know what they like to do on their days off from the church. Ask the pastor, in a positive spirit, why he feels led to preach what he preaches. Ask the minister of music about which songs he likes best and why. Ask the minister of education about his goals for growing the church in Sunday school and Discipleship Training? Fourth, provide value to their ministry with words of encouragement to them and by speaking to other church members positively about their ministry. Fifth, you should acknowledge their position, understanding they too are servants of God, and that they have been sent by God to serve the people of the church of which you are a part.

You should spend time on Saturday night praying for your pastor and staff, that they may minister under the anointing of the Holy Spirit on Sunday. Be quick to defend them as they minister under God's leadership. Never permit anyone to defame them or their family's character falsely. Speak out to church members on their behalf concerning their family's financial needs, remembering, "the labourer is worthy of his hire" (Luke 10:7). Tell them and others when their ministry is a blessing to you. Everyone I have ever met wants to be loved and appreciated. So does your pastor and staff. They are not a pawn to be used, but a servant of the Lord that can and does enhance the worship and growth of a church. Their primary responsibility is to lead the church from point A to point B. To do their work, the pastor and staff members need the support of the deacons and other church leaders.

Some deacons believe it is their responsibility to supervise the pastor and staff. This is not a deacon's responsibility, and they should not assume that role. When a church has several staff members, there should be a personnel committee to administer and make recommendations concerning the needs of the staff, under the direction of the pastor.

What about your sexual purity?

One of the greatest struggles for many today is maintaining purity in a sex-saturated society. What once was confined to adult bookstores is now openly displayed on television. Many motels and hotels now provide R- and X-rated movies. Our schools, instead of promoting abstinence and chastity, encouraged the use of contraceptives and help students acquire them without parental consent. I am of the opinion that the problem of sexual immorality occurs in America today because of:

1. A love for the world and the things of the world
2. A desire to satisfy the flesh!
3. An absence of respect for the Word of God
4. A failure of the pulpit to preach the whole counsel of God
5. A flagrant disregard for the sovereignty of God

Satan has convinced some that they are so involved into sexual immorality that they cannot be forgiven. However, Paul tells us that Satan is a liar because ". . . we have redemption through [Christ's] blood, the forgiveness of sins, according to the riches of his grace" (Eph. 1:7). Satan has convinced others, "they are only human—no one is perfect—it is just impossible to say no to sexual immorality." I have heard men say, "I have tried to stop thinking about illicit sex, but I can't." Peter has a word to say about this:

> Wherefore gird up the loins of your mind, be sober, and hope to the end for the grace that is to be brought unto you at the revelation of Jesus Christ; as obedient children, not fashioning yourselves according to the former lusts in your ignorance: But as he which hath called you is holy, so be ye holy in all manner of conversation; because it is written, Be ye holy; for I am holy. And if ye call on the Father, who without respect of persons judgeth according to every man's work, pass the time

of your sojourning here in fear: Forasmuch as ye know that ye were not redeemed with corruptible things, as silver and gold, from your vain conversation received by tradition from your fathers; but with the precious blood of Christ, as of a lamb without blemish and without spot.

—1 Peter 1:13-19

It is amazing how Satan can use lust to destroy a man's ministry. Having been in upward of eight hundred churches since entering evangelism, I have heard many stories about deacons, pastors, and staff members being involved in sexual impropriety. Paul instructs the members of the church at Thessalonica to "Abstain from all appearance of evil" (1 Thess. 5:22). As a deacon, you are an example for others. You are the only Christ some know and the only Bible some read. It is impossible to live in sin without eventually being discovered. The consequences for sexual sin are damaging to the individual, his family, his church, and the cause of Christ. Paul's challenge to the Christians at Thessalonica is applicable for Christians today. Paul says in 1 Thessalonians 4:1-3:

Furthermore then we beseech you, brethren, and exhort you by the Lord Jesus, that as ye have received of us how ye ought to walk and to please God, so ye would abound more and more. For ye know what commandments we gave you by the Lord Jesus. For this is the will of God, even your sanctification, that ye should abstain from fornication.

How is your sexual relationship with your wife? Is it pleasing to God? If there are problems, what are you doing about them? Have you and your wife ever sat down and discussed what you want and need in your sexual relationship from each other. Such a discussion demands an understanding of the difference between men and women. The fact that men and women are different is demonstrated at every stage of life. Men are physical, women are emotional. Watch boys at play. They play games that are physical; games of contact. Girls, on the other hand, play nurturing games. Games that mimic being a mother and caring for a baby. Men and women talk differently! When girls begin to talk, they use sentences to express themselves. Boys, however, most often use phrases like "whoa" and "yeah!" Most adult women talk more than adult men do. Women are more prone to talk face to face with each other. Men are reluctant to address other men in this fashion, preferring to talk to one another at a distance and without much eye contact. Have you ever been at a gathering of men and women and heard some woman say, "Do any of you ladies need to go to the bathroom?"; and a good number of women get up and go? You will never hear a man ask that question, and if one does, then he will not be invited to the next gathering.

Ask a young boy what he wants to be when he grows up, and he will tell you an occupation. He wants to be a firefighter, a policeman, et cetera. Ask a young girl what she wants to be when she grows up, and she will tell you a relationship. She wants to be a wife or a mother. Ask an adult male who he is, and he will tell you his name and give you his occupation. Ask an adult woman who she is, and she will tell you her name and give you her relationships. "I am Jane Doe, the wife of Bill Doe and the mother of . . ." and she will tell you her children's names and ages. Men and women are different!

Men think about sex differently than women. Men are excited sexually by the physical—sight, touch and smell. Women are excited sexually by the emotional—soft tender words, gentle caresses, and words of love. The last session of the marriage retreat that I conduct deals with the question, "What do you do when the fire goes out in your marriage?" My answer is, "You find the wood, feed the fire, and fan the flame!" First, you find the wood. If a married couple wants their sexual relationship to improve, they must discover the proper kindling to place on their mate's fire. Just any stick won't do. What will fire up a man's fire sexually will not fire up a woman's fire sexually. How do you determine what "wood" you need to place on your mate's fire? You ask them! Ask, "What can I do for you that will make our sexual relationship better?"

Second, you feed the fire! You write down what they want—not what you want, but what they want—and you do what they ask. This does not mean that you are to participate in un-Christian acts of immoral sexual behavior. As Christians, believing that God created sex as the climax of love in the bond of marriage, it is reasonable to believe that sex is wholesome, healthy, and enjoyable. Sex, therefore, should be given its proper place in marriage. Likewise, your mate should know the wood that you request for your fire and be willing to provide it, as you provide what she wants for her fire.

Third, you fan the flame! Anyone knows you don't build a fire in the fall and expect it to last all winter. Wood must be placed on the fire continuously if the fire is to continue to burn. Simply speaking, a couple's sex life requires continuous care and attention! Listen again to what Paul says about a husband and wife's sexual relationship:

> Let the husband render unto the wife due benevolence: and likewise also the wife unto the husband. The wife hath not power of her own body, but the husband: and likewise also the husband hath not power of his own body, but the wife. Defraud ye not one the other, except it be with consent for a time, that ye may give yourselves to fasting and prayer; and come together again, that Satan tempt you not for your incontinency.
>
> —1 Corinthians 7:3-5

Paul informs married couples that the husband and wife are to submit themselves to each other sexually. Neither the husband nor the wife should be dishonest with each other in their decision not to engage in sexual activity. When a couple refrains from sexual intercourse, it should be done by consent and for a legitimate reason and only then for a reasonable period of time to prevent Satan from tempting them.

What about the change you can provide as an individual through your church?

Could you say that your church is accomplishing all God would have it accomplish? A common statement made by many in the church today is, "I am just one person! How can I make a difference in my church?" The needs of your church and your community might seem overwhelming. You might feel like there is no point trying to do anything. You may wonder how one person can make a difference in what needs to be done?

Look back across the pages of the Bible and note how many men and women made a great contribution to their society by the way they lived. Noah was just one man, yet look what he did for God. As he labored for one hundred and twenty years, there was little outward evidence of success. He was mocked and ignored. I am sure he became discouraged and often wondered if he was doing God's will. Yet, he remained faithful! His faithful service has been an inspiration to millions down through the years. Ladies, look at the life of Esther. Her faithfulness saved her people from the actions of Haman. Esther's Uncle Mordecai reminded her of something you may need to hear today. He told Esther, ". . . and who knoweth whether thou art come to the kingdom for such a time as this?" (Esther 4:14).

When I was pastor of the Ebenezer Baptist Church in Columbia, Alabama, the church began to grow, and we soon needed more space. A good number of our members expressed their interest in a new educational building. As time passed, Mr. Harvey Taylor, a deacon who had experience with building construction asked if he could lead this project. Mr. Taylor organized a series of meetings with those who would be using the educational building; and from these meetings, plans for the new building were formulated and approved by the church. He took it upon himself to go to individual families within the church and solicit the funds to buy the materials for the new building. When the materials were purchased, he organized volunteer laborers from within the church and personal friends he knew from the community, and the building was soon built. Mr. Taylor made a difference.

Mrs. Anita Angel was the W.M.U. director at the Angel Grove Baptist Church in Jacksonville, Alabama. Not long after I became pastor, Anita came to me and said, "Brother Don, I am ashamed of our Sunday school building. I can't remember the last time it was painted. Our church is reaching more people than we ever have, and some of us are ashamed of the way our church looks." I asked her what she had in mind. She said, "I want to challenge the W.M.U. and our church to paint the inside of our Sunday school building." I asked her to present her proposal to the church in the following conference. She said, "Our church has a policy that forbids women from making or seconding a motion in conference. However, once a motion is made, a woman can ask questions or express her view." I asked her to find two men, one who would make the motion and another who would second the motion. When the motion was presented to the church in the following conference, Anita stood and shared her challenge to the church! The church liked her idea and recommended that new drapes and new carpet also be purchased and placed in the Sunday school building. Soon the Sunday school building looked as good as new.

It wasn't long until some of the other women in our church were expressing their opinions about how bad the sanctuary looked in comparison to the redecorated Sunday school building. Soon, the two contractors and their crews, who were members of our church, were busy remodeling the sanctuary and expanding the parking lot. For the first time in a long time Angel Grove Baptist Church had a new look. Not only was the church remodeled, but, for the first time in its history, the church had central air conditioning. All of this came about because one woman had a desire for change.

Mr. Dave Manzo was a member of the Liberty Baptist Church in College Park, Georgia. Dave was a mechanic for Delta Airlines in Atlanta. When our church started a bus ministry, Dave assumed the responsibility for keeping the buses mechanically fit. Dave worked on the busses most afternoons and virtually every Saturday. Year after year, despite the weather or his own fatigue, Dave remained faithful. His service made it possible to bring many people to church and to Christ.

What would God have you do through your church? You don't have to be a builder or a painter or a mechanic. If you and one more man in your church would win one soul to Christ every other week, your church could baptize twenty-six people in a year. If your wife and a female friend joined in this venture, your church could baptize fifty-two in a year. If you were able to encourage others to share their faith; if you could encourage one family to tithe, one family to attend Sunday and Wednesday evening worship services, one husband to become the spiritual leader in his home, you would do your church and your friends a great service. Do not assume you cannot do great things for God! One of your primary responsibilities as a deacon is to encourage other church members to do more for Christ. I want to challenge you and your wife to pray, asking the Lord to place some specific needs your church has on your heart. I also want to challenge you and your wife to set some goals that will help you meet those needs. Needs will never be met in our churches, if everyone waits on someone else to address them.

As you have examined yourself, what would you say about your spiritual condition? What would you say about your ministry as a deacon or a deacon's wife? Are you doing your best for the cause of Christ? Do you really believe you are a blessing to your church? What, if anything, do you need to change in your life as a deacon or as a deacon's wife?

Printed in the United States
217564BV00001B/2/P

9 781607 917106